The Principles of Sufism

Letter from the General Editor

The Library of Arabic Literature series offers Arabic editions and English translations of significant works of Arabic literature, with an emphasis on the seventh to nineteenth centuries. The Library of Arabic Literature thus includes texts from the pre-Islamic era to the cusp of the modern period, and encompasses a wide range of genres, including poetry, poetics, fiction, religion, philosophy, law, science, history, and historiography.

Books in the series are edited and translated by internationally recognized scholars and are published in parallel-text format with Arabic and English on facing pages, and are also made available as English-only paperbacks.

The Library encourages scholars to produce authoritative, though not necessarily critical, Arabic editions, accompanied by modern, lucid English translations. Its ultimate goal is to introduce the rich, largely untapped Arabic literary heritage to both a general audience of readers as well as to scholars and students.

The Library of Arabic Literature is supported by a grant from the New York University Abu Dhabi Institute and is published by NYU Press.

Philip F. Kennedy
General Editor, Library of Arabic Literature

About this Paperback

This paperback edition differs in a few respects from its dual-language hardcover predecessor. Because of the compact trim size the pagination has changed, but paragraph numbering has been retained to facilitate cross-referencing with the hardcover. Material that referred to the Arabic edition has been updated to reflect the English-only format, and other material has been corrected and updated where appropriate. For information about the Arabic edition on which this English translation is based and about how the LAL Arabic text was established, readers are referred to the hardcover.

The Principles of Sufism

BY

ʿĀʾishah al-Bāʿūniyyah

TRANSLATED BY

Th. Emil Homerin

FOREWORD BY

Ros Ballaster

VOLUME EDITOR

Shawkat M. Toorawa

NEW YORK UNIVERSITY PRESS

New York and London

NEW YORK UNIVERSITY PRESS
New York and London

Library of Congress Cataloging-in-Publication Data
Bā'ūnīyah, 'Ā'ishah bint Yūsuf, -1516 or 1517, author.
[Muntakhab fī uṣūl al-rutab fī 'ilm al-taṣawwuf. English]
The Principles of Sufism / 'A'ishah al-Bā'ūniyyah ; translated by
Th. Emil Homerin.
pages cm
Includes bibliographical references and index.
ISBN 978-1-4798-2924-8 (pb : alk. paper) — ISBN 978-1-4798-2491-5 (e-book) —
ISBN 978-14798-6468-3 (e-book)
1. Sufism—Early works to 1800. I. Homerin, Th. Emil, 1955-, translator. II. Title.
BP188.9.B39 2016 (print) / BP188.9 (ebook)
297.4/1—dc23 2015042457 (print) / 2015044609 (ebook)

New York University Press books are printed on acid-free paper,
and their binding materials are chosen for strength and durability.

Series design and composition by Nicole Hayward
Typeset in Adobe Text

Manufactured in the United States of America

10 9 8 7 6 5 4 3 2 1

In memory of

Farouk Mustafa

dedicated teacher, master translator, respected colleague,
and a very kind man

"To live in hearts we leave behind is not to die."

Thomas Campbell

Contents

Foreword

ROS BALLASTER

> "Praise God, who pours His aid upon His beloved ones as a special allotment and reward, quenching their hearts from the drink of oneness with love and purity, revealing Himself to their inner hearts in glory and beauty, and gracing them with gifts of proximity in contemplation and union. I praise Him with the praise of one to whom He made Himself known. Then she knew and was blessed with his grace, and confessed and acknowledged that this was beyond all thanks. I bear witness that there is no deity but God, alone without peer. This is the witness of one who roamed in the deserts of singularity and drowned in the ocean of oneness. Then she turned her gaze from creation and witnessed the True Reality by means of the True Reality."

These are the stirring words which introduce 'Ā'ishah al-Bā'ūniyyah, scholar and poet, to her readers. They are the words of a woman passionately in love whose beloved has completed and, most important of all, oriented her being. She was lost and he "turned her gaze" to what is real and true. The solid reality she now inhabits is, however, not to be seen in the created world, nor is it accessible to those without her revelation.

So 'Ā'ishah witnesses for her readers this truth through an instructional book that speaks through metaphor: she provides substitutes in language for a truth beyond representation. Those substitutes derive from the tradition she inherits and has studied with the passionate attention her attachment demands. *The Principles of Sufism* is a mystical guide book drawing lessons and readings from the Sufi tradition. Sufism is represented here as a tree with lots of branches but four essential roots: repentance, sincerity, recollection, and love. Each of these principles is addressed in a separate section of the book and each of those sections quotes a number of prophetic traditions to demonstrate the writer's learning at the same time as it mediates her understanding. She progresses by citing early Muslim forebears, then later Sufi masters, and concludes with her own observations and poetic verses. Thus, her own voice is grounded, founded, indeed *rooted*, in the words of others.

This is then what we might call a "performative" linguistic act in which the work itself enacts or performs each stage it describes. I came to the *Principles of Sufism* as a reader well-versed in the traditions and allusions of the western (largely Christian) literary tradition. Like 'Ā'ishah, I inevitably sought out parallels and terms I know to arrive at an informed and sympathetic relationship to a world otherwise strange to me. Comparative reading is always of course a reaching to what seems familiar as a way of understanding the strange. So here, I thought immediately of the tradition of English mysticism in the prophetic writings and speech of Christian women from the medieval accounts of Margery Kempe (*The Book of Margery Kempe*, composed in the 1430s) and Julian of Norwich (*Revelations of Divine Love*, composed ca.1395) through to the millenarian prophetesses of the seventeenth century, such as Elinor Channel (*A Message from God, by a Dumb Woman* of 1654) and Eleanor Davies (who composed some seventy prophetic pamphlets in the 1620s and 1630s). For me, 'Ā'ishah's work had most resonance with Anna Trapnel's *Cry of a Stone: or a Revelation of Something Spoken in Whitehall* of 1654. Although Trapnel's work is her speech reported by an amanuensis, and its only textual reference is the books of the Bible, it shares with 'Ā'ishah's writings that intense focus on a witness to an identity set alight through encounter with the divine. It seeks to bring about that same ignition and animation in its audience. Anna, like ʿĀʾishah, refers to herself in the third person in order better to figure that capacity to mediate divinity. Anna speaks directly to her God only to announce that He speaks through her: "thy servant is made a voice, a sound, it is a voice within a voice, even thy voice through her."

The turning of the self away from self and away from the material world to respond to an imperative call to subject oneself to a God is the pattern of the mystic and one especially powerful and enabling for women. Both Anna and ʿĀʾishah use the metaphor of material and natural objects made to speak (the cry of the stone) by the encounter with the divine. The promise is to achieve a higher oneness and a new differentiation from the everyday and from ties to those who lack this revelation (those who drown in the ocean of oneness rather than find their place within it). Such mystical seizure legitimates a refusal of the domestic and the everyday, and a turn to "inwardness" which is characterized as an opening up of the self to a more powerful and demanding "authority" than any other, God. Mystics often represent that inward turn in powerfully material terms, especially as a form of "feeding" or "drinking." Strangely enough, in contemplating ʿĀʾishah's ways of figuring the Sufi path (obviously deeply conventional), I had a flash to Lewis Carroll's heroine, Alice, responding to those imperatives to eat and drink as an attempt to satisfy her curiosity about a perplexing world in which she seeks some new kind of understanding. ʿĀʾishah offers powerful and attracting metaphors drawn from material elements and physical experience of the principles she is invoking: repentance is "a fire in the heart that flares up and a rift that never mends" (§1.15); sincerity is "red sulphur. If an ounce of it were thrown on a ton of copper deeds, it would turn them into pure gold fit for a king" (§2.25); remembrance is like selecting the sweetest dates to eat (§3.25).

ʿĀʾishah's writing is, however, significantly different from the words of the women prophets of the western Christian tradition, who often deliver autobiography and criticize temporal forms of government. There is no further mention of 'Ā'ishah's femaleness after her opening statement. Indeed, she provides no further biographical information and no self-reference beyond demonstrating the depth and complexity of her learning. In this respect the text reads more like a kind of conduct book or instructional work than prophetic revelation. Her experience is exemplary not specific; her gender is not, it appears, material to the story of her union with God. Conversely, there is an impressive confidence here. 'Ā'ishah does not see the male mystics she cites and quotes as having any more authority more than her own. She evidences none of the uncomfortable struggle with male priests and authority figures that we see in the works of Christian women in Europe of the same period.

I found myself seeking in *The Principles of Sufism* for 'Ā'ishah's own words, her poetry unmediated through those of others on the nature and experience of love. And then I thought again. It seems to me that much of what 'Ā'ishah has to say is a refusal of self; words are not the "property" of their speaker or writer—they are a witness of others' words, and her aim is to provide a textual palimpsest which leads her reader toward her God, not toward the author. God is destination and origins must be effaced (even if the sources of words are acknowledged). I thought here of that complex moment in John Bunyan's allegory of the Christian life, *The Pilgrim's Progress* of 1678, in which we first meet Christian, after a visitation from Evangelist, fleeing his home and family in a desperate pursuit of the real life with God and salvation:

> "Now, he had not run far from his own Door, but his Wife and Children perceiving it, began to cry after him to return; but the Man put his fingers in his Ears, and ran on, crying, Life, life, Eternal life: so he looked not behind him, but fled towards the middle of the Plain."

It is unsurprising that the devotional literatures of the world's monotheisms—Islam, Judaism, and Christianity—should resonate with each other, not least in the call to subject oneself absolutely to a divine alterity. However, it is worth noting some differences, especially for women in their pursuit of this kind of fulfilment. 'Ā'ishah has a much less problematic relation to learning and indeed publishing than her western counterparts. Anna Trapnel was literate but her revelations are scribed by a male amanuensis. Anna does not, however, mediate her understanding of the divine through the words of other thinkers and learned men. There is much to celebrate in 'Ā'ishah's unproblematic demonstration of learning. This is a tradition that is in many ways *very* different and unassimilable to western literary traditions which, even in the most postmodern of moments, are preoccupied with originality and invention. *The Principles of Sufism* provides for the woman reader seeking the voice of women in history an instructive example beyond its own intent pursuit of theological truth: we read and see here a woman who communicates her literary sensibility and creativity through acts of translation and mediation of the words of others, who defies our expectations of literary property and "origin-ality" to show us just how urgent, fresh and liberating the encounter with the voices of the past can be.

Ros Ballaster
Professor of Eighteenth-Century Studies
Faculty of English Language and Literature
Mansfield College, University of Oxford

Abbreviations

Ar.	Arabic equivalent
ca.	*circa*, approximately
d.	died
EI	*Encyclopaedia of Islam*, 1st edition.
EI2	*Encyclopaedia of Islam*, 2nd edition
EI3	*Encyclopaedia of Islam Three*, 3rd edition
EQ	*Encyclopaedia of the Qur'an*
fl.	flourished
r.	ruled

Acknowledgments

This project has taken shape over a number of years, and has had the support of many institutions and foundations. I am grateful for the support of the Fulbright Foundation, the National Endowment for the Humanities, the American Research Center in Egypt, and the University of Rochester. In Egypt, I was greatly assisted by Dār al-Kutub al-Miṣriyyah, the Netherlands-Flemish Institute in Cairo, the American University in Cairo, and the American Research Center in Egypt. I would also like to acknowledge the dedicated work of the editors of the Library of Arabic Literature, especially Tahera Qutbuddin and Shawkat Toorawa, who proofread the entire manuscript and made valuable corrections and suggestions. I also wish to thank a number of friends and colleagues who have also graciously given me their support for this project, including Fatima Bawany, Daniel Beaumont, Kenneth Cuno, Bruce Craig, Li Guo, Aḥmad Harīdī, Carl Petry, Marlis Saleh, John Swanson, Edward Wierenga, and, with love, Nora Walter.

Introduction

ʿĀʾishah al-Bāʿūniyyah (d. 923/1517) was an exceptional Muslim scholar. She was a mystic, and a prolific poet and writer, composing more works in Arabic than any other woman prior to the twentieth century. In her writings, ʿĀʾishah often speaks of her abiding love for God and His prophet Muḥammad, and her quest for mystical union. These concerns are central to *The Principles of Sufism*, a mystical guide book that ʿĀʾishah compiled to help others on this spiritual path. Drawing lessons and readings from a centuries-old Sufi tradition, ʿĀʾishah advises the seeker to repent of selfishness and turn to a sincere life of love. Fundamental to this transformation is the recollection of both human limitations and God's limitless love. In *The Principles of Sufism*, ʿĀʾishah recounts important stages and states on the path toward mystical union, as she urges her readers to surrender themselves to God and willingly accept His loving grace.

Life

ʿĀʾishah al-Bāʿūniyyah was born in Damascus in the second half of the fifteenth century AD. She came from a long line of religious scholars and poets, originally from the small village of Bāʿūn in southern Syria. In search of education and employment, members of the Bāʿūnī family eventually made their way to Damascus, and for several generations, they served the Mamlūk sultans of Egypt and Syria. ʿĀʾishah's father Yūsuf (d. 880/1475) was a scholar of Shāfiʿī jurisprudence and rose to prominence as the chief judge in

Damascus. He made sure that all of his children received a fine education, and so ʿĀʾishah, together with her five brothers, studied the Qurʾan, the traditions of the prophet Muḥammad, jurisprudence, and poetry.[1] ʿĀʾishah mentions that she had memorized the entire Qurʾan by the age of eight, and that, as a teen or young woman, she went with her family on the Hajj pilgrimage, during which she had a vision of the prophet Muḥammad:

> God, may He be praised, granted me a vision of the Messenger when I was residing in holy Mecca. By the will of God the Exalted, an anxiety had overcome me, and so I resolved to visit the holy sanctuary. It was Friday night, and I reclined on a couch on an enclosed veranda overlooking the holy Kaaba and the sacred precinct. It so happened that a man there was reading a poem on the life of God's Messenger, and voices rose with blessings upon the Prophet. Then, I could not believe my eyes—it was as if I was standing among a group of women. Someone said, "Kiss the Prophet!" and a dread came over me that made me swoon until the Prophet passed before me. So I sought his intercession and, with a stammering tongue, I said to God's Messenger, "O my master, I ask you for intercession!" Then I heard him say calmly and deliberately, "I am the intercessor on the Judgment Day."[2]

As part of her education, ʿĀʾishah also studied Sufism, which was the general practice of the Bāʿūnī family. One of her great uncles had been a Sufi ascetic, while another uncle had been the director of a Sufi chantry in Damascus. Moreover, members of the Bāʿūnī family, including ʿĀʾishah's father, were buried in a family plot near the lodge of the Sufi master Abū Bakr ibn Dāwūd (d. 806/1403). This shaykh was affiliated with the ʿUrmawī branch of the Qādiriyyah Sufi order to which the Bāʿūnī family belonged, and in a number of her writings, ʿĀʾishah specifically praised her two Qādirī masters, Jamāl al-Dīn Ismāʿīl al-Ḥawwārī (d. 900/1495), and his successor, Muḥyī al-Dīn Yaḥyā al-ʿUrmawī (fl. eleventh century/sixteenth century):

> My education and development, my spiritual effacement and purification, occurred by the helping hand of the sultan of the saints of his time, the crown of the pure friends of his age, the beauty of truth and religion, the venerable master, father of the spiritual axes, the axis of existence, Ismāʿīl al-Ḥawwārī, may God sanctify his heart and be pleased with him, and, then, by the helping hand of his successor in spiritual states and stations, and in spiritual proximity and union, Muḥyī al-Dīn Yaḥyā al-ʿUrmawī, may God continue to spread his ever-growing spiritual blessings throughout his lifetime, and join us every moment to his blessings and succor.[3]

The Bāʿūnīs were a prominent family in Damascus, so ʿĀʾishah married a man known as Ibn Naqīb al-Ashrāf, the son of another distinguished family there who were descendants of the prophet Muḥammad. ʿĀʾishah's husband's full name was Aḥmad ibn Muḥammad Ibn Naqīb al-Ashrāf (d. 909/1503), and he, too, was a devotee of shaykh Ismāʿīl al-Ḥawwārī. ʿĀʾishah and Aḥmad had at least two children together: a son, ʿAbd al-Wahhāb (897–925/1489–1519), and a daughter, Barakah (born 899/1491). In AD 1513, ʿĀʾishah, by then a widow, left Damascus for Cairo with her son to seek a job for him in the Mamlūk administration. En route, bandits ambushed their caravan in the Egyptian delta and stole everything, including all of ʿĀʾishah's books. As a result, ʿĀʾishah and her son were destitute when they arrived in Cairo, but they received the assistance of a family friend, Maḥmūd ibn Muḥammad ibn Ajā (d. 925/1519), the foreign minister and confidential secretary of the Mamlūk sultan, al-Ghawrī (r. 906–22/1501–16). Ibn Ajā generously provided for them and employed ʿĀʾishah's son as a secretary in the chancellery.

ʿĀʾishah spent the next three years in Cairo where she studied jurisprudence with a number of scholars. She graciously accepted Ibn Ajā's financial support, for which she praised him in several poems, and she continued to write and compose new works. Then, in AD 1516, ʿĀʾishah left Cairo with her son, who had been assigned to accompany Ibn Ajā to Aleppo. There, the Sultan al-Ghawrī was preparing for war against the Ottomans to the north, yet he took the time to hold a personal audience with ʿĀʾishah. ʿĀʾishah then returned to her native Damascus, where she died soon thereafter in AD 1517. Our sources do not tell us why al-Ghawrī met with ʿĀʾishah, though al-Ghawrī was quite fond of Arabic poetry, and so was probably familiar with ʿĀʾishah's poetic reputation. It is also possible that the sultan sought ʿĀʾishah's spiritual blessings for his trials ahead, for it is quite apparent from accounts of ʿĀʾishah al-Bāʿūniyyah by her contemporaries that she was highly regarded as a pious woman and Sufi master.[4]

Thought and Work

As an educated Muslim woman, ʿĀʾishah al-Bāʿūniyyah was privileged, but she was by no means unique within medieval Muslim society. Throughout the Middles Ages, there was a significant number of educated Muslim women, though few of them wrote original works. ʿĀʾishah al-Bāʿūniyyah was truly exceptional for having composed over a dozen works of prose and poetry, praised by a number of her contemporaries. Today, many of ʿĀʾishah's writings are lost, but we know from surviving manuscripts and from her own statements that much of her work addressed mystical themes and praised the prophet Muḥammad.[5] ʿĀʾishah composed a number of laudatory accounts of Muḥammad's life and prophetic career (*mawlids*), which combined prose and poetry. In fact, celebration of the Prophet appears to have been ʿĀʾishah's vocation, perhaps undertaken, in part, thanks to her vision of him while on pilgrimage. ʿĀʾishah also composed a considerable amount of verse, including two collections of poetry that still survive. One, simply entitled *The Collected Verse of ʿĀʾishah al-Bāʿūniyyah* (*Dīwān ʿĀʾishah al-Bāʿūniyyah*), which ʿĀʾishah composed during her stay in Cairo, contains six long poems praising the prophet Muḥammad. Among them is an ode incorporating al-Būṣīrī's (d. 694/1295) celebrated panegyric to Muḥammad, *The Mantle Ode* (*al-Burdah*),[6] and ʿĀʾishah's most famous poem, *Clear Inspiration in Praise of the Trusted Prophet* (*al-Fatḥ al-mubīn fī madḥ al-Amīn*). This latter work is a *badīʿiyyah*, a complex type of poem popular during the Mamlūk period, which praises the Prophet while illustrating various rhetorical schemes (*badīʿ*) used in Arabic verse. ʿĀʾishah composed one hundred and thirty verses for her *Clear Inspiration*, each containing a praiseworthy attribute or action of the Prophet illustrated by a rhetorical device (e.g., antithesis, alliteration). ʿĀʾishah consciously patterned this long ode on similar poems from earlier poets of the Mamlūk period, and she further displays her extensive knowledge of Arabic verse in her commentary on the poem in which she refers to nearly fifty earlier poets.[7]

The second surviving collection of ʿĀʾishah's verse is entitled *Emanation of Grace and the Gathering Union* (*Fayḍ al-faḍl wa-jamʿ al-shaml*) and contains over 370 poems, spanning ʿĀʾishah's mystical life from her "days as a novice and student, to her mastery of the branches of mystical annihilation and the arts of effacement."[8] In her introduction to this collection, ʿĀʾishah notes that many of these poems were inspired by God and represent intimate conversations with Him regarding spiritual states and mystical matters. Nearly every poem is preceded by the phrase, "From God's inspiration upon her," and in many instances, this is followed by a few additional words regarding the poem's composition, such as "when rapture was intense," or "from His inspiration upon her during a session of mystical audition."[9] Such autobiographical information for poems is rare in any literary tradition, yet ʿĀʾishah al-Bāʿūniyyah wished to share aspects of her mystical life with her readers.

In many of the later poems in *Emanation of Grace*, ʿĀʾishah confidently assumes the role of the Sufi master who guides the spiritual novice, and this shift is clear in one of her longest poems in the collection. Composed of 252 verses and modeled on Ibn al-Fāriḍ's (d. 632/1235) Sufi classic *Poem of the Sufi Way* (*Naẓm al-sulūk*), ʿĀʾishah's long ode takes up a number of similar Sufi themes.[10] Both poems rhyme in the letter "t" and praise the wine of love, spiritual intoxication, and union with the divine Beloved. ʿĀʾishah also follows Ibn al-Fāriḍ when she invokes the "ancient covenant" as the original source of her love for God. In Sufi circles, this phrase refers to the "Day of the Covenant" (*yawm al-mīthāq*) alluded to in the Qurʾan (Q Aʿrāf 7:172):

> «And when your Lord drew from the loins of the children of Adam their progeny and made them bear witness against themselves: "Am I not your Lord?" They said, "Indeed, yes! We so witness . . ."»

ʿĀʾishah al-Bāʿūniyyah, Ibn al-Fāriḍ, and many other Sufis believed that God called forth humanity to take this covenant prior to creation, thus bringing about the original loving encounter between the divine spirit within each human being, and God. Recollection of this moment is thought to result in the annihilation of selfishness and the spirit's return to abide lovingly in God's oneness.

The Principles of Sufism

In her verse, ʿĀʾishah al-Bāʿūniyyah often alludes to Sufi teachings, which she attempts to elucidate in her prose writings on Sufism. Those of her works that survive give us an idea of the mystical influences on her, which include al-Nawawī's (d. 676/1277) book on prayer, *The Book of Recollections* (*Kitāb al-Adhkār*); al-Jurjānī's (d. 816/1413) Sufi lexicon, *The Book of Definitions* (*Kitāb al-Taʿrīfāt*), and al-Anṣārī's (d. 481/1089) spiritual guidebook, *Stages for the Wayfarers* (*Manāzil al-sāʾirīn*). Additional important sources for ʿĀʾishah's mystical ideas and teachings are most readily apparent in the Sufi guidebook she composed entitled *al-Muntakhab fī uṣūl al-rutab fī ʿilm al-taṣawwuf*. Loosely rendered as *The Principles of Sufism*, a more exact translation is *Selections on the Principles of the Stations in the Science of Sufism*. "Selections" refers to ʿĀʾishah's many quotations that form the basis of this book, drawn from the Qurʾan, hadith collections, Qurʾanic commentaries, spiritual guidebooks, hagiographies, and mystical epistles by earlier Sufi masters, including al-Kalābādhī (d. 380/995), al-Sulamī (d. 412/1021), and especially, al-Qushayrī (d. 465/1074). ʿĀʾishah also quotes a number of later Sufi authorities, including Ibn al-ʿArīf (d. 536/1141), ʿUmar al-Suhrawardī (d. 632/1234), and Ibn ʿAṭāʾ Allāh al-Iskandarī (d. 709/1309).

In the *Principles of Sufism*, ʿĀʾishah compares Sufism to a tree with many branches, yet having four essential roots or principles: repentance (*tawbah*), sincerity (*ikhlāṣ*), recollection (*dhikr*), and love (*maḥabbah*). She discusses each principle in detail in separate sections, beginning each section with relevant verses from the Qurʾan, along with Sufi commentaries on them. She then quotes a number of prophetic traditions, carefully noting her sources in most instances, demonstrating once again her extensive religious education and erudition. Next, ʿĀʾishah cites aphorisms by early Muslim forbearers (*salaf*), and then sayings, teachings, and stories of later Sufi masters. ʿĀʾishah concludes each section by integrating this material with her own observations on the subject and poetic verses inspired by God.

Throughout *The Principles of Sufism*, ʿĀʾishah al-Bāʿūniyyah follows in the classical Sufi tradition by stressing God's omnipotence, while affirming that the all-powerful God is also all-merciful and forgiving. A person seeking God's favor must repent and discipline selfish human nature, so that God's grace may be seen within the heart. Then, the believer can cultivate a sincere devotional life to God and serve humanity based on love. An essential means to attain and maintain a religious life of love is remembrance of God. ʿĀʾishah quotes God's vow in the Qurʾan (Q Baqarah 2:152): «Remember Me, and I will remember you,» urging the seeker to pray and remember God often. In the Sufi tradition, remembrance also refers to the practice of meditation on God, which may lead to mystical union with Him. ʿĀʾishah regards remembrance as both a process and a mystical state. As a process, remembrance of God is a way to purify oneself of selfishness and hypocrisy, and a means to ward off Satan. As a mystical state, remembrance differs in its effects depending on the believer's spiritual level; common people are calmed and blessed by praising God, while religious scholars who think about God gain theological insight into His nature. By contrast, the practice of remembrance among the spiritually advanced mystics leads to their purification and a tranquil state in God. For a powerful remembrance, 'Ā'ishah recommends that seekers recite and meditate on the declaration of faith found in the Qur'an (Q Muḥammad 47:19): «There is no deity but God!»[11]

In *The Principles of Sufism*, 'Ā'ishah singles out verses from the Qur'an and traditions from Muḥammad regarding God's love of humanity and His promise to forgive the sins of those who repent. 'Ā'ishah urges all sincere believers to love God, His prophet Muḥammad, and fellow believers. Significantly, for those graced by God, this love will eradicate selfishness and even the sense of self, as God overwhelms them in union with Him. 'Ā'ishah reinforces this point with a saying popular among the Sufis known as the "Tradition of Willing Devotions":

> God said, "My servant draws near to Me by nothing more loved by Me than the religious obligations that I have imposed upon him, and My servant continues to draw near to Me by acts of willing devotion such that I love him. Then, when I love him, I become his ear, his eye, and his tongue; his heart and reason; his hand and support."[12]

'Ā'ishah states that love is God's greatest secret; it is an endless sea without a shore which many people and religions of the past have tasted, but none more so than the most blessed of all creation, the prophet Muḥammad, and his spiritual, saintly descendants (*awliyā'*, lit. "protected friends"). God has transformed them and all those He loves by means of a mystical experience beyond description. Their hearts then become places of spiritual vision where the truth of the divine essence is revealed. As love draws seekers ever closer to their divine Beloved, God bestows His love as an act of unearned grace. Ultimately, the lovers lose all sense of self when the truth of oneness appears, and their mystical death leads them to the bliss of eternal life, as 'Ā'ishah declares in verse at the end of *The Principles of Sufism*,

> God looked with favor on a folk,
> so they stayed away
> from worldly fortunes.
> In love and devotion, they worshipped Him;
> they surrendered themselves
> with the best intention.
> They gave themselves up to Him
> and passed away from existence
> with nothing left behind.
> Then with kindness and compassion,
> He turned to them
> and revealed to them His essence.
> And they lived again
> gazing at that living face
> as His eternal life appeared.

A Note on the Text

This English translation of *The Principles of Sufism* is based on *al-Muntakhab fī uṣūl al-rutab fī ʿilm al-taṣawwuf*, manuscript 318 (Taṣawwuf Taymūr) in Cairo's Dār al-Kutub al-Miṣriyyah, and dated 1071/1661. ʿĀʾishah's writings have been carefully read and copied in Arabic for centuries, and so they deserve a reasonable counterpart in English. Further, when translating her verse, I have been concerned not only with a poem's form and content, but also with its tones, moods, and deeper meanings. Toward this end, my own method of translation generally follows that laid out by Robert Bly in *The Eight Stages of Translation*.[13] All translations, including of the Qur'an, are my own. Dates are generally cited in their Islamic/Ḥijrī year followed by their Common Era equivalent: e.g., 923/1517.

Notes to the Introduction

1 This account of the life and work of ʿĀʾishah al-Bāʿūniyyah is drawn from Homerin, "Living Love," 211–16, and *Emanations*, 11–27.

2 ʿĀʾishah al-Bāʿūniyyah, *Mawrid*, 104–5; also quoted in Rabābiʿah, *ʿĀʾishah al-Bāʿūniyyah*, 53.

3 Ibn al-Ḥanbalī al-Ḥalabī, *Durr al-ḥabab*, 1:2:1063–64.

4 Homerin, "Writing," 396–97.

5 For a tentative list of ʿĀʾishah's works, see Homerin, "ʿĀʾishah al-Bāʿūniyyah."

6 ʿĀʾishah al-Bāʿūniyyah, *Qawl*.

7 ʿĀʾishah al-Bāʿūniyyah, *Fatḥ*.

8 ʿĀʾishah al-Bāʿūniyyah, *Dīwān Fayḍ al-faḍl*, 326.

9 ʿĀʾishah al-Bāʿūniyyah, *Dīwān Fayḍ al-faḍl*, 73, 193.

10 ʿĀʾishah al-Bāʿūniyyah, *Dīwān Fayḍ al-faḍl*, 237–51, and Homerin, *Emanations*, 96–139.

11 For more on ʿĀʾishah's views on remembrance, see Homerin, "Recalling."

12 See Schimmel, *Mystical Dimensions*, 43.

13 Bly, *Eight Stages*, 13–49.

The Principles of Sufism

In the Name of God, the Merciful and Compassionate, Who suffices me. 0.1

Praise God, who pours His aid upon His beloved ones as a special allotment and reward, quenching their hearts from the drink of oneness with love and purity, revealing Himself to their inner hearts in glory and beauty, and gracing them with gifts of proximity in contemplation and union. I praise Him with the praise of one to whom He made Himself known. Then she knew and was blessed with His grace, and confessed and acknowledged that this was beyond all thanks. I bear witness that there is no deity but God, alone without peer. This is the witness of one who roamed in the deserts of singularity and drowned in the ocean of oneness. Then she turned her gaze from creation and witnessed the True Reality by means of the True Reality. I bear witness that the most special of the special ones, the master of the messengers, the chosen of the chosen ones, the most eminent of creation is His most praiseworthy Muḥammad, His most glorious emissary, His dearest beloved, and His noblest friend. May God bless and cherish him with prayers for all eternity, abiding in perpetuity, with prayers that will continue to bring us aid and instruction from him. May God also bless his brethren among the prophets and emissaries, all of his family and companions, all progeny, and all the righteous. May He give them eternal peace and exalt them! 0.2

0.3 When the sincerity to seek grew strong in one of the dear friends, and he stood waiting at the door with his head on the doorsteps, God revealed to us the purity of his heart and the sincerity of his intention, and we observed that, thanks to the grace of God, he was one of those filled with the gifts of divine providence and marked by mercy for the realization of Lordly love. We saw him looking longingly for instruction in the way of realization and for guidance to the right path. So we sought God's guidance, may He be glorified, for explaining things to him in the language of speech that he might, if the exalted God so wills, attain the language of the mystical state. Then we answered his request and fulfilled his hopes solely for the grace of God and His satisfaction, for all aid and right guidance are from Him. He is my sufficiency and «the best trustee»![1]

0.4 Know, may God show you mercy, that the stations of the Sufi folk, God's people, are innumerable, but their branches have four roots from which each station spreads, namely: repentance (*tawbah*), sincerity (*ikhlāṣ*), remembrance (*dhikr*), and love (*maḥabbah*). We will discuss each of these four principles based on what we have found in the Qur'an and in the prophetic traditions, as well as the knowledge we have acquired about the true state of affairs among the Sufi folk replete with subtle allusions. I have named this *The Principles of Sufism*. Assistance comes from God, and protection is with God. With His aid and care, may He keep this work free of errors, and may it be a benefit to others.

The First Principle: Repentance (*Tawbah*)

God the Exalted has said, «Turn to God, together, O believers, that you might be successful.»[2] The Exalted has said, «Seek forgiveness from your Lord, then turn to Him in repentance,»[3] and the Exalted has said, «O you who believe, turn to God with sincere repentance!»[4] The Exalted has said, «And those who do not turn in repentance, they are the transgressors!»[5] and the Exalted has said, «Truly God loves those who turn in repentance, and He loves those who purify themselves.»[6] There are similar sayings in the noble verses of the Qur'an. 1.1

According to the lexicons, *tawbah* means "to return." *Tāba*, *āba*, and *anāba* all have one meaning, which is "return." *Thāba* is similar; people say, "The milk returned (*thāba*) to the udder." Outward repentance is the return from blameworthy actions to praiseworthy ones and from foul words to righteous ones. Inner repentance, with which the Sufi folk are concerned, is to turn away from all things and toward God, mighty and glorious. Repentance is not valid without three things: remorse for sin, abstention from it, and the resolution not to return to it.[7] When one of these conditions is not met, repentance is not valid.[8] This is the rule for repentance for sin between the servant and His Lord. 1.2

In the case of sins against another created being, such as injustice, slander, and the like, repentance requires additional conditions 1.3

such as giving just compensation, seeking forgiveness from the one slandered, and so forth. One should then strive to be free of liability as much as is possible by compensation, by settling accounts, and by seeking forgiveness.[9] If one is unable to do that, then one should persist in seeking God's help for remission of sins. When God, may He be glorified, knows that His servant is sincere, He forgives him, and He reconciles him with his debtors by means of His beneficence and generosity.

1.4 There are many hadiths about repentance. Anas ibn Mālik, may God be pleased with him, related as follows: "The Emissary of God, God bless and cherish him, said, 'If the servant turns in repentance for his sins, God will cause the recording angels to forget his sins, and will obliterate any remnant or mark of his sin from the earth, such that, on Judgment Day, there will be no one to bear witness against him before God the Exalted regarding any sin.'" Abū l-Shaykh al-Iṣbahānī reports this. Also Anas, may God be pleased with him, related that the Prophet, God bless and cherish him, said, "Every human being is a wrongdoer, but the best of the wrongdoers are those who turn in repentance." This is reported by al-Tirmidhī and Ibn Mājah.[10] ʿAbd Allāh ibn Masʿūd, may God be pleased with him, related that the Prophet said, "The Garden of Paradise has eight gates; seven are bolted tight while the open gate is for repentance until the sun rises in the west on Judgment Day." This is reported by Abū Yaʿlā and al-Ṭabarānī, with an excellent chain of authorities.

1.5 Abū Hurayrah, may God be pleased with him, related that the Emissary of God, God bless and cherish him, said, "Were you to commit wrongs such that your sins rose up to the sky, and then you turned in repentance, God would turn to you with forgiveness!" This is reported by Ibn Mājah. Abū Hurayrah, may God be pleased with him, related as follows: "The Emissary of God, God bless and cherish him, said, 'When the believer commits a sin, a black spot appears in his heart. If he turns in repentance, desists, and asks forgiveness, the spot will be polished away. But if it has grown so large that it envelops his heart, then it is like the rusting that God the mighty and glorious mentions when He says, «What they earned rusted their hearts.»'"[11] This is reported by al-Tirmidhī, who says the report is sound.

1.6 Ibn Mas'ūd, may God be pleased with him, related that the Prophet, God bless and cherish him, said, "The one who turns from sin is like one who never sinned." This is reported by Ibn Mājah and al-Ṭabarānī. Abū Hurayrah, may God be pleased with him, related that the Emissary of God, God bless and cherish him, said, "God mighty and glorious said, 'I am with My servant when he thinks of Me, and I am with him whenever he recollects Me.' By God, God is more pleased with the repentance of His servant than any of you who is pleased to find his stray animal in the desert. God said, 'One who draws near Me by a hand span, I draw near him by an arm's length, and one who draws near Me by an arm's length, I draw near him by the span of open arms, and if he walks toward Me, I run to him!'" This is reported by Muslim.

1.7 Abū Dharr, may God be pleased with him, related that the Emissary of God, God bless and cherish him, said, "One who does good for the rest of his life, God forgives him for what has passed, but one who does evil for the rest of his life, God will hold him to account for what has passed and for what is yet to come." This is reported by al-Ṭabarānī with an excellent chain of authorities. 'Uqbah ibn 'Āmir, may God be pleased with him, related that the Emissary of God, God bless and cherish him, said, "The person who does bad deeds and then does good deeds is like a man wearing a tight coat of chain mail that is suffocating him. When he does something good, a link loosens. Then he does another good deed, and another link loosens, and so on until he can step out free into the world." This is reported by the Imām Aḥmad ibn Ḥanbal. Abū Dharr and Mu'ādh ibn Jabal, may God be pleased with them both, related that the Prophet, God bless and cherish him, said, "Fear God as much as you can and follow a bad action with a good deed, and treat people with kindness." This is reported by al-Tirmidhī, al-Ḥākim, and al-Bayhaqī.

1.8 Anas, may God be pleased with him, related that the Prophet, God bless and cherish him, said, "'Shall I tell you about your disease and your cure?' 'Yes, Emissary of God!' we said, and he replied, 'Your disease is sin, and your cure is seeking forgiveness.'" The Prophet, may God bless and cherish him, also said, "One who seeks forgiveness with his tongue while persisting in his sin is like one who mocks his Lord!" There are similar things in the noble hadiths, but we have related what should suffice one whom God has blessed with success.

1.9 There are many statements on repentance by the pious forbearers. Fuḍayl ibn ʿIyāḍ said, "To seek forgiveness of God without desisting from sin is the repentance of the impostors!"[12] Yaḥyā ibn Muʿādh al-Rāzī said, "If you do not believe in the Last Day, you are a hypocrite, and if you persist in sin, you are lost!" Rābiʿah al-ʿAdawiyyah, may God be pleased with her, used to say, "Our seeking forgiveness requires asking for it time and time again!"[13] Ubayy ibn Kaʿb, may God be pleased with him, said, "God, may He be praised and exalted, has said, 'I do not like it when a wrongdoer dies with his wrong, or a criminal with his crime. But, if one turns to Me and repents, My Garden is vast, My mercy broad, and My hands are open wide, for I am the most merciful of those who give mercy!'" Luqmān said to his son, "Do not put off repentance, for death comes suddenly."[14] Ṭalq ibn Ḥabīb said, "Truly, what is due to God is beyond what servants can offer, so turn for forgiveness in the morning and evening."[15]

1.10 Ibrāhīm al-Tayyimī said, "I imagined my soul in the Garden, and it was as if I were eating the food of Paradise and embracing my wives there. Then, I imagined my soul as if I were in Hell, chained in fetters and eating from its bitter Zaqqūm tree. So I said to my soul, 'Which do you desire?' and it replied, 'I will return to the world and repent!' I said, 'And what of you, since I asked you the question? Get up now and repent!'" ʿUmar ibn al-Khaṭṭāb, may God be pleased with him, said, "Sit with the penitents; surely they have the most refined of hearts."[16] Yaḥyā ibn Muʿādh al-Rāzī said, "One slip for a penitent after his repentance is more odious than seventy before it."[17]

1.11 As for the Sufi folk, God's people, their discussion of repentance is extensive and limitless, and absolutely true concerning repentance. Ruwaym, may God be pleased with him, said, "The meaning of repentance is that you turn away from repentance," that is, from the regard for repentance and attention to it, since attention to something other than God is a veil.[18] Al-Nūrī said, "That is, you turn away from everything except God the Exalted."[19] ʿAbd Allāh ibn ʿAlī al-Tamīmī Abū Naṣr al-Sarrāj said, "What a difference there is between the penitent who repents of moral lapses, the penitent who repents of heedless things, and the penitent who repents of regard for his good deeds."[20]

1.12 When asked about repentance al-Ḥusayn al-Maghāzilī said, "Are you asking me about turning to God in repentance or turning to Him in deference?" The questioner replied, "What is turning to Him in repentance?" and he said, "That you fear His power over you." The questioner asked, "Then what is turning to Him in deference?" and he said, "That you are ashamed before God the Exalted because of His nearness to you."[21] This second turning is higher than the first since renouncing sin out of fear of retribution is merely seeking good fortune and only done for one's self. However, renouncing sin out of shame before one's exalted Lord to glorify His lordship, is higher and nobler since turning in shame proves true the servitude by which one exalts Him.

1.13 Abū ʿAlī al-Daqqāq said, "Repentance has three stages: the first is repenting, the second is turning toward God, and the final part is returning to God. Therefore, repenting is the beginning, turning is the middle, and returning is the end. Thus one who repents out of fear of retribution has repented, and one who repents for a reward has turned to God. As for the one who turns out of deference to the divine command, neither out of desire or out of fear, he has returned." This is a summary of what the master Abū l-Qāsim al-Qushayrī relates.[22]

1.14 Dhū l-Nūn al-Miṣrī said, "The repentance of the common people is for sin. The repentance of the people of spiritual distinction is for heedlessness, and the repentance of the prophets is for regarding the weakness of others who fail to attain what they did." Ibrāhīm al-Daqqāq said, "Repentance is that you face God without turning your back on Him, whereas before, you used to turn your back on Him and never faced Him."[23] This means that you devote yourself to Him, shunning everything but Him.

1.15 It has been said that repentance is remorse for what has passed and clinging to what is pure. Some say that repentance is moving away from what God has forbidden toward what God has commanded. It has been said that repentance is devotion to the True Reality and shunning created things, and that repentance is sincerity, seeking refuge, and striving persistently with hope. It has been said that repentance is feeling shame when one makes a mistake, and that repentance is sorrow for what has passed. Some say that repentance is the return to God the Exalted in every instant, thought, and glance, and that repentance is shame that restrains one from sin, and constant tears of remorse. It has been said that repentance is removing the garment of estrangement and donning the garment of fidelity. Some say that repentance is the return from blameworthy attributes to praiseworthy attributes, which can only be brought about by seclusion, by holding one's tongue from useless talk, and by eating lawful food. It has been said that repentance is a fire in the heart that flares up, and a rift that never mends.[24]

1.16 The master Abū l-Qāsim al-Qushayrī relates the following, with his chain of authority from al-Junayd who said,

> I met al-Sarī one day, and I saw that he was upset. "What's wrong?" I asked, and he replied, "A young man came to me and asked about repentance. So, I said to him, 'It is that you do not forget your sins.' But he disagreed with me and said, 'It is that you *do* forget your sins!'" I replied to al-Sarī, "As I see it, the young man spoke the truth," and al-Sarī said, "How so?" and I replied, "If I am in the mystical state

> of estrangement, and He moves me to the state of purity, then memory of estrangement in the state of purity would be estrangement."

Abū Naṣr al-Sarrāj said, "Al-Sarī alluded to the repentance of the novices, which is in a state of flux, while al-Junayd alluded to the repentance of the spiritually realized ones; they do not recollect their sins because their hearts are overwhelmed by the majesty of God and the constant remembrance of Him."[25]

It is said that God ordered a type of repentance for every kind of person: the disobedient are to return to obedience, and obedient persons are to turn away from concern for obedience and toward seeing success. For the chosen elite, however, repentance is to turn away from seeing success to contemplate Him who gives success. It is also said that He ordered all to repent lest a penitent person should feel ashamed of repenting by himself. Thus, He the Exalted has said, «Turn to God, together, O believers, that you might be successful.»[26] God, may He be praised, ordered repentance so that they might benefit from it, not so that their obedience be an embellishment for Him, may He be praised.[27] 1.17

Abū Yazīd al-Bisṭāmī said, "Turning from sin occurs once, but from obedience, a thousand times."[28] Al-Qushayrī said, "Were it not that God the Exalted turns in forgiveness to the worshipper, the worshipper would never ever repent."[29] 1.18

Know, may God show you mercy, that every part of the body has a share in repentance. Thus for the heart, there is the intention to avoid sin, and remorse; for the eye, there is lowering one's gaze; for the hand, there is refraining from grabbing; for the foot, there is giving up running to prohibited places; for the ear, to stop listening to useless prattle, and so forth.[30] This is the repentance of the common people. The repentance of the people of distinction is all this, plus opposing concupiscent desire, lowering the heart's gaze away from all good fortune, and renouncing the ephemeral world. This is the repentance required for the love of God the 1.19

Exalted, described in His saying: «Truly, God loves those who turn in repentance.»[31]

1.20 The repentance of the chosen elite is for looking at anything but God, for attachment to anything other than God, for reliance on anything but God, and for being occupied with anything other than God. This repentance includes everything, even proximity to God, religious practices, mystical states, miracles, and mystical ranks and stations—everything except God the Exalted—such that one's turning in repentance is by one's Lord and to one's Lord. This is the purest destination, the highest station in repentance, for it is a branch from the root of repentance pertaining to his honorable Muḥammadian majesty when the Exalted says, «He forgave the Prophet.»[32]

1.21 One of the great scholars has said, "In the above verse from the Qur'an, He alludes to the repentance of the one who never sinned, as a pretext for those who do sin, by calling attention to the fact that no member of the community of the Prophet, God bless and cherish him, enters a station without following his example." One of the people of spiritual realization said that mention of repentance in this verse is the removal of the clot from Muḥammad's noble breast by angels,[33] and some say that this clot was Satan's portion. Therefore, it is as if he, may God bless and cherish him, sought forgiveness for Satan's evil ever having been inside him. Another has said this verse is a precedent for the repentance of the Prophet's community such that, by this precedent, the outcomes of the penitents' repentance will be valid. Someone said, "The repentance of the prophets is for seeing creation at the time of being called to prophecy since they are never absent from the divine presence, for they are always in the center of union."[34]

1.22 Sahl al-Tustarī said, "Of the rights due to God in this world below, none is more necessary for humanity than repentance, and there is no worse retribution than loss of repentance."[35] Ibn Manṣūr said,[36] "Repentance is the effacement of human nature and the confirmation of divinity, such that you return to the root of nonexistence, while the True Reality abides as ever." This small portion of the subtle allusions of the Sufi folk should be sufficient for one to whom God gives success.

It is important to add as an appendix to this principle, the finest divine sayings and choicest of authoritative stories. Success comes from God alone! Al-Ḥasan al-Baṣrī, may God be pleased with him, related as follows: 1.23

> When God turned in forgiveness to Adam, on whom be prayers and peace, the angels congratulated him, and Gabriel and Michael descended to him and said, "Adam, rejoice for the forgiveness upon you from God mighty and glorious!" "Gabriel," he replied, "if a question remains after being forgiven, it is, 'What is my status?'" God the Exalted then revealed to him: "O Adam, you have bequeathed toil and trouble to your progeny, but I have bequeathed repentance to them. Whoever among them prays to Me, I will respond to him, and whoever asks Me for forgiveness, I will not withhold it from him, for I am near, and I answer, O Adam. I will gather the penitents from the graves on Judgment Day, and they will be happy and laughing, and their prayers will be answered!"[37]

It is related that when the sinner shuts the door, lowers the cur- 1.24
tain, closes the window, and gets down to sin, the earth will say, "O Lord, allow me to swallow him up!" and the sky will say, "Allow me to fall upon him!" The glorious and exalted Lord will reply, "If the servant is your servant, then do with him what you will. But if he is My servant, then leave him alone. For if he comes to Me in the darkest of night, I will accept him, and if he comes to Me in the brightest of day, I will accept him. There is no gatekeeper or warden blocking My door, and whenever he comes to Me, he will find a path. Whenever he calls, 'My Lord?' I answer, 'My servant!' and whenever he says, 'I have sinned, O, Lord!' I reply, 'I have forgiven you, My servant!'"[38]

1.25 In one of the stories of the Israelites, mighty and glorious God says, "O child of Adam, you are not fair to Me. I remember you, but you forget Me. I call you to Me, but you run away from Me. I keep misfortunes away from you, yet you are addicted to sin. O child of Adam, you will have no excuse tomorrow when you come to Me on Judgment Day. Woe to you, if these words do not sting you! Know that you are in grave danger! Take heed of yourself or be prepared for the painful chastisement!"[39]

1.26 Dhū l-Nūn al-Miṣrī said, "God the Glorious revealed the following to Moses, peace be upon him:"

> Be like the solitary bird who eats from the treetops and drinks from clear water, and when night descends upon it, takes shelter in one of the caves, settling down with Me and averse to any who disobey Me. O Moses, I have promised Myself not to bring to fruition any action by someone who works against Me, and I will cut asunder anyone who hopes for other than Me; I will break the back of anyone who relies on other than Me; I will prolong the agony of anyone who is intimate with any other than Me, and I will abandon anyone who loves a lover other than Me! O Moses, I have servants who whisper intimately to Me, so I listen to them, and when they call Me, I turn to them. If they approach Me, I come near to them, and if they come near to Me, I embrace them. If they befriend Me, I bring them close; if they are sincere to Me, I am sincere toward them, and if they strive toward Me, I reward them. I am the ruler of their affairs, the governor of their hearts, and the power over their mystical states. I do not allow their hearts to repose in anything but remembrance of Me, for they are intimate with Me alone. They bring their hearts before Me, alone, and their abode is made only in My shelter.[40]

1.27.1 Abū l-Fayḍ Dhū l-Nūn al-Miṣrī, may God be pleased with him, related as follows:

I was told about a man from Yemen. I departed on pilgrimage to the Holy House of God in Mecca, and when I finished the Hajj, I sought out this man that I might listen to his words and profit from his spiritual counsel. There were people with me seeking blessings as I was, including a young man who had the mark of righteousness and the look of those who are fearful of God; his face was sallow, though not from illness, and he was bleary-eyed, though not from inflammation. He loved seclusion and being alone, as if he were close to his appointed time. We used to reproach him for keeping to himself and ignoring us, but that only made him struggle all the more. As has been said:

Blamers of love, go easy;
I can never replace my love of him.
How can I forget him since my passion flared,
and I gave up my honor for shame?
"You're being tested," they said. Indeed my bones
are worn away in the grave, though love of you never fades!
For I drank love of you within my heart
since I was a child in ancient times.

That young man stayed with us until we arrived in Yemen. There, we asked after the home of the shaykh, and we were directed to it. We knocked on his door, and he came out to us as if he had been brought news of the dead. We sat with him, and the youth greeted him and said a few words. Then the shaykh took his hand and welcomed him with glad tidings, but not us, though we had also greeted the shaykh. The young man drew near him and said, "O my master, God the Exalted has made you and those like you physicians for the hearts and healers of the diseases of sin. I have a festering wound and a disease, that has spread and will not respond to treatment. If you see fit to give me one 1.27.2

of your remedies, do so please!" Then the shaykh recited to him:

Sin's disease! What an awful disease!
How can I be saved from my sin's disease?
Is there a physician to counsel me?
The doctors and all humanity are powerless to treat me.
O my shame and bitter grief from standing
when I come to stand before my Lord,
Cut off from His answer to my prayers—and why not?—
with my distress beyond description![41]

1.27.3 Again, the young man said to the shaykh, "If you see fit to give me one of your remedies, please do so!" The shaykh replied, "Ask what you want," and the youth said, "What is the sign of fear?" "That fear of God causes you to renounce fear of anything but Him," answered the shaykh. The youth shuddered and fell unconscious for an hour. When he recovered, he said, "May the exalted God show you mercy! When can the servant be certain that his fear is of God the Exalted?" and the shaykh replied, "When he relegates himself in this world below to the state of a sick man, such that he refuses any food for fear of prolonging the illness, while bearing patiently the medicine's agonizing effects for fear of prolonging his wasting away."[42] Then the young man screamed, and we thought that his spirit had departed, but then he said, "May God show you mercy! What is the sign of love for God the Exalted?" and the shaykh replied, "My dear one, the rank of love for the exalted God is sublime!" and the young man said, "Describe it!" "My dear one," the shaykh replied, "God pulls away the veil from the hearts of His lovers, and they see, by the heart's light, the glory of the Beloved's majesty. Their spirits become holy, their hearts are illuminated, and their intellects become heavenly. They see only the Beloved, and their lot is only union!"

At that, the young man groaned and died, may God have mercy upon him. The shaykh began to turn him over, saying, "This is the death of those who fear God; this is the rank of the lovers. This is a spirit who yearned and moaned, who listened and grew noble, then screamed and died."[43] As someone has said: 1.27.4

The more a man knows, the greater his fear,
for no one knows God without fearing Him.
One who feels safe from God's designs is ignorant of Him,
while one who fears God's designs knows Him.[44]

Mālik ibn Dīnār, may God be pleased with him, related as follows: 1.28.1

One day, I saw a young man who had the diffidence of repentance and the light of one whose prayers are answered. Tears were streaming down his face. Then I recognized him as someone I used to know as blessed with wealth and good fortune. I cried when I saw him in this state, and he cried when he saw me. He greeted me and said, "O Mālik, cling to God, for you certainly remember how I was during the good times. Perhaps God will have mercy upon me and forgive me!" Then he recited:

Mention me if Zaynab will listen and say,
"His thoughts are never free of you for an instant!"
If she hears mention of me, perhaps she'll say,
"How is that friend of yours?"

Mālik said: 1.28.2

Then he turned and left, weeping. The pilgrimage months arrived, and I set out for Mecca. While I was in the Sacred Mosque, I saw a circle of people around a young man who had thrown himself down and had interrupted the pilgrims in their circumambulation of the Kaaba with his profuse weeping. I stopped with the others to look at him, and it was my former companion. I was glad to see him, so I greeted him and said, "Praise God who has exchanged your fear of Him with His protection and given you what you desired!" Then he began to recite, may God show him mercy:

Without fear,
    they travelled safely to Khayf,
        and when they alighted at Minā,
    they attained their desires.
They had hopes,
    so He gave them their desires
        and protected them with His forgiveness,
    completely free of indecency and obscenity.
The cupbearer of the folk
    circled among them with wine,
        and when they called out, "Who bears the cup?"
    He said to them, "I do!"
"I am God, so call on Me,
    for I am your Lord!
        Mine are the glory and majesty,
    the praise and sovereignty!"[45]

1.28.3 Mālik said:

I said to him, "By God, tell me what's happened to you," and he replied, "It has only been good. God called me with His grace, and I answered Him, and so He gave me all that I sought from Him!" Then he recited:

When He called me, I said, "Welcome! Come in!"
    In union with You, how sweet is Your love, how fresh!
By Your reality, You are the goal, the wish, the desire,
    and when the blamer blames me for loving You and goes on and on,
My heart does not long for the Arak trees of Naʿmān,
    nor for Khayf or Qubā's land.
If they appeared one day with Suʿdā or Zaynab,

I would not long for Su'dā, no, nor desire Zaynab.
For whenever those encampments are recalled, O my masters,
then my goal above all others is she who lives in the tent there.[46]

Mālik said, "Then he went back to his circumambulation of the Kaaba, and he left, and I never saw him again or heard news of him."

Fuḍayl ibn 'Iyāḍ said, "While standing on the Plain of 'Arafāt during the Hajj, I saw a quiet young man marked by meekness and humility. As the people around us were praying to God to fulfill their needs, I said, 'Young man, hold your hands before your heart and pray for your needs,' and he replied, 'Master, melancholy has come upon me, and now I have no time.' 'If this is so, it is too late,' I replied, and he said to me, 'Indeed.' 'Indeed,' I agreed, and when he tried to raise his hands, he screamed and fell dead." 1.29

The case of Ibrāhīm ibn Adham's repentance is well known. He was a descendent of the kings of Khurasan. He went out to hunt, and flushed out a fox, or perhaps a rabbit, and as he pursued it, the voice of an invisible guide spoke to him: "You were not created for this; you were not commanded to do this!" Then a voice spoke from his saddle bow: "By God, you were not created for this; you were not commanded to do this!" So he dismounted his horse and came upon one of his father's shepherds. Ibrāhīm took the shepherd's cloak, which was made of wool, and put it on, and he gave the shepherd his clothes, gear, and horse. He then went to Mecca, and the rest is history.[47] 1.30

The cause of Shaqīq al-Balkhī's repentance has also been related. He was the scion of a wealthy family, who, as a young man, traded in the land of the Turks. There, he entered a temple full of idols, and when he saw their caretaker, Shaqīq said to him, "Truly, you have a God, a creator, living, omniscient, and omnipotent. Believe in Him and not these idols, which can do no harm nor good." "If it is as you say," replied the caretaker, "then He should be able to provide 1.31

for you in your own country so that you would not need to trouble yourself to come here for trade." Shaqīq understood and, after repenting, took to the path of renunciation, and the rest is history.[48]

1.32 By God, these are the distinguishing marks of the sincere penitents. The subtlest expression, the slightest allusion, is enough to drive them away from anything other than God; they have no concern nor business except Him. «They are the party of God! Will not the party of God be the successful ones?»[49]

1.33 Know, may God show you mercy, that when God the Exalted wants to befriend one of His servants, He opens the door of repentance for him with His grace, and leads him into the anteroom of renunciation of all but Him. God raises him up with the ascension of vigilance against any except Him until he ends up in the presence of contemplation, where He seats him on the carpet of proximity with the generosity of attraction, and manifests Himself to him in beauty. Then what was not, is annihilated, and what always was, abides. «There, the protection of God, the True Reality, is the best reward and the greatest success!»[50] When the seed of repentance falls on the ground of the heart, and the breezes of remorse blow, and the clouds of the eyelids pour with the rain of tears, then that earth «will tremble, sprout, and grow verdant with delightful species»[51] of the flowers of epiphanies and the harvest of contemplation, from the aromatic plants of union and the fruits of communion, and so on from what is beyond description and expression.

1.34 When God turns to a servant with forgiveness, He causes the recording angels to forget what they recorded of the servant's bad deeds; He exchanges his bad deeds for good, and registers him among His beloved ones. When the lamentations of His dear servant rise, God boasts about him to the angels. God's love is especially for the penitents, as the Exalted has said, «Truly God loves those who turn in repentance!»[52] Suffice for the penitent the honor that he is God's beloved.

1.35 If you do not turn to God in repentance, you will have no success. You must therefore validate your repentance with hard work.

Repentance is the foundation for the pillars of happiness. The servant will enter the Sufis' mystical stages only through the door of repentance, and he will attain his goal only by holding fast to repentance. Your forefather Adam, peace be upon him, with all of his prestige, still fell from the abode of felicity into the abode of misery due to sin. Then what of your condition? «Does the human being reckon that he will be left alone?»[53] Never! «Every man is held accountable for what he earned.»[54] The procrastinator will soon be taken by surprise, and when he sees his punishment, he will say, «Would that I had a second chance, I would be one of those who do good!»[55] Do not suppose that a delay in judgment is a blessing while you persist in sin. No, indeed! It is the harshest reckoning, as God the Exalted has said, «We give them a respite that they may increase in sin.»[56]

We ask God for forgiveness, and we ask Him to bless us and you with the repentance of the sincere, the turning back of those who know, and the return of those who profess the unity of God by His grace and generosity, for He «is the most merciful of those who show mercy!»[57]

How aptly someone said:

Though my sins grow great and oppressive,
 Your forgiveness of sins is greater still.
Yet as Your mercy holds me here,
 I will need it more at the Resurrection!

God has inspired these verses of mine on this subject:[58]

Though my grave faults sicken my condition,
 my faith in Your grandeur is strong indeed.
Though the wide world closes in on me for my sin,
 good thoughts of You are boundless indeed.

Here are more verses inspired by Him:

Sound opinion relayed to me
 a prophetic tradition, not prattle,

That You are merciful and kind,
  sweeping in forgiveness.
Master, prove my thoughts true
  quenching my thirst with generosity,
And erase all that You have written down
  of my sins.
For Your promise of redemption is confirmed by words
  related from the Prophet who spoke true
That You are with the servant who thinks of You,
  so the One is there to protect him![59]

1.40 This is what God has inspired as a discourse on the first principle of repentance. Success comes from God alone!

The Second Principle: Sincerity (*Ikhlāṣ*)

God the Exalted has said, «Worship God sincerely, dedicating faith to Him alone.»[60] He has said, «Say, "I was ordered to worship God sincerely, dedicating faith to Him alone."»[61] He the Exalted has said, «They were ordered only to worship God sincerely, dedicating faith to Him alone.»[62] 2.1

Ibn 'Abbās, may God be pleased with both him and his father, said, "In the Torah and the Gospel, people were commanded only to worship God sincerely, professing His oneness." 2.2

Ibn 'Umar, may God be pleased with both him and his father, related as follows: "I heard the Emissary of God, God bless and cherish him, say, 2.3.1

> Three men from before your time set out on a journey and sought shelter in a cave for the night. As they entered, a boulder rolled down the mountain and trapped them in the cave. They said to one another, 'We will only be saved if we appeal to God based on the righteousness of some deed.' One of them said, 'Dear God, my parents were very old, and I used to give them the evening drink of milk first, before my own wife, children, and slaves. Once, I was delayed, and when I came to my parents, they were asleep. I milked my animals for their evening drink, but I found my parents still sleeping. I was loathe to give the milk to

my family or slaves before them, so I stayed, cup in hand, waiting for them to wake until dawn broke. [Some of those reporting this tradition add, "And the children were yelping at my feet."] Then my parents awoke, and they drank their milk. Dear God, if I did this for Your sake, remove from us this boulder before us!' Then the boulder moved slightly, but not enough for their escape.

2.3.2 "The Prophet, God bless and cherish him, continued,

The second one said, 'Dear God, my uncle had a daughter whom I loved more than any other person. I wanted her, but she refused me. Then, some years later, I visited her, and I offered her one hundred and twenty dinars if she would let me have my way with her. She agreed, but as I was about to mount her, she said, "You are not permitted to take my virginity unless you marry me!" I got off and left, though I loved her more than any other person, and I left the gold. Dear God, if I did that for Your sake, remove from us this boulder before us!' Then the boulder moved, but not enough for their escape.

2.3.3 "The Prophet, God bless and cherish him, continued,

The third one said, 'Dear God, I hired a group of workers and gave them their wages, except for one man who had left without collecting them. I invested his wages, and the wealth grew considerably. After a time, he came to me and said, "O servant of God, give me my wages." I replied, "All that you see here—camels, cattle, sheep, slaves—is from your wages," and he said, "O servant of God, don't mock me!" "I am certainly not mocking you," I replied. So he took them all and herded them off, leaving nothing behind. Dear God, if I did this for Your sake, remove this boulder before us.' Then the boulder moved, and they walked out."

This is reported by al-Bukhārī, Muslim, and al-Nasā'ī. Ibn Ḥibbān also reports it in his *Sound Traditions* (*Ṣaḥīḥ*) in summary fashion from a tradition from Abū Hurayrah.

Al-Ḍaḥḥāk ibn Qays, may God be pleased with him, related as follows: "The Emissary of God, God bless and cherish him, said, 'Blessed and exalted God has said, "Anyone who attributes a partner to Me belongs to that partner!" O people, dedicate your deeds with sincerity, for God, blessed and exalted, does not accept any deed unless it is dedicated sincerely to Him. Do not say this is for God and kin. For then it is for kin, and none of it is for God. Do not say this is for God and yourselves. For then it is for yourselves, and none of it is for God.'" Al-Bazzār reports this with an acceptable chain of authorities, and al-Bayhaqī relates it as well. 2.4

Abū Saʿīd al-Khudrī, may God be pleased with him, related that the Prophet, God bless and cherish him, said the following during the Farewell Pilgrimage: "God grants a good life to any person who has heard my words and memorized them. Many a person carries knowledge without being an expert. Three things are always found in the heart of a believing man: sincerely dedicating one's deeds to God, counseling Muslim leaders, and adhering to the community of Muslims, for their prayers embrace those who stand behind them." Al-Bazzār reports this with a good chain of authorities. Thawbān, may God be pleased with him, related that the Emissary of God, may God bless and cherish him, said as follows: "Blessed are the sincere ones, for they are the lamps of guidance that dispel all the trials of darkness." This is reported by al-Bayhaqī. 2.5

Muʿādh ibn Jabal, may God be pleased with him, related that when he was to be sent to Yemen he said, "O Emissary of God, please advise me," and the Prophet replied, "Be sincere in your faith and even a few good deeds will suffice you." Al-Ḥākim reports this, and he said that it had a sound chain of authorities. Abū l-Dardāʾ, may God be pleased with him, related that the Prophet, God bless and cherish him, said the following: "This world is cursed, and all that is in it is cursed, except what has been done for the sake of God the Exalted." This is reported by al-Ṭabarānī. ʿUbādah ibn al-Ṣāmit, may God be pleased with him, reported that the Prophet said, "When Judgment Day comes to this world, the order will be given: 2.6

'Separate out the things here that belong to God!' Those will be set aside, and all else will be thrown into Hellfire." This is reported by al-Bayhaqī.

2.7 'Umar ibn al-Khaṭṭāb, may God be satisfied with him, related as follows: "I heard the Emissary of God, God bless and cherish him, say, 'All acts are judged on intentions, and every person will receive what he intended. Whoever emigrated for God and His Emissary, his emigration is to God and His Emissary. Whoever emigrated for gain in this world or to marry a woman, then his emigration was for that.'" This is reported by al-Bukhārī, Muslim, Abū Dāwūd, al-Tirmidhī, al-Nasā'ī, and others. Abū Umāmah related as follows: "A man came to the Emissary of God, God bless and cherish him, and said, 'What about the man who fought, seeking reward and fame? What does he receive?' and the Emissary of God, God bless and cherish him, replied, 'He receives nothing.' The questioner repeated this question three times, and the Emissary of God, God bless and cherish him, responded, 'He receives nothing.' Then he added, 'God does not accept any action unless it is sincerely dedicated to Him alone for His sake.'" This is reported by Abū Dāwūd and al-Nasā'ī with an excellent chain of authorities. Abū Hurayrah, may God be pleased with him, related as follows: "The Emissary of God, God bless and cherish him, said, 'People will be resurrected based only on their intentions.'" Ibn Mājah reports this with a good chain of authorities.

2.8 Abū Hurayrah, may God be pleased with him, reported as follows: "The Emissary of God, God bless and cherish him, said, 'God does not look at your bodies or your shapes. Rather he looks into your hearts.'" This is reported by Muslim. Abū Hurayrah also said, "I heard the Emissary of God, God bless and cherish him, say,

> The first person to be judged on the Day of Resurrection will be a man who was martyred. He will be brought forward and informed of the blessings he received, and he will acknowledge them. God will say, 'What did you do to deserve them?' and the man will reply, 'I fought for Your

> sake until I was martyred.' God will say, 'You lie! You only fought so that people would say, "He is courageous!" and so they did.' Then the orders will be given, and the man will be dragged away face down until he is thrown into Hell. Next will be a man who acquired knowledge, taught it, and read the Qur'an. He will be brought forward and informed of the blessings he received, and he will acknowledge them. God will say, 'What did you do to deserve them?' and the man will reply, 'I acquired knowledge, taught it, and read the Qur'an for Your sake.' God will say, 'You lie! You only acquired knowledge so that people would say, "He is a scholar!" and you only read the Qur'an so that they would say, "He is a Qur'an reader!" and so they did.' Then the orders will be given, and the man will be dragged away face down until he is thrown into Hell. Next will be a man to whom God was generous, giving him all kinds of wealth. He will be brought forward and informed of the blessings he received, and he will acknowledge them. God will say, 'What did you do to deserve them?' and the man will reply, 'I always followed the path that You love of distributing wealth to others, and I gave only for Your sake.' God will say, 'You lie! You only distributed wealth to others so that people would say, "He is a generous man!" and so they did.' Then the orders will be given, and the man will be dragged away face down until he is thrown into Hell."

This is reported by Muslim and al-Nasāʾī, and it is also reported by al-Tirmidhī and Ibn Ḥibbān in his *Sound Traditions*, both with identical wording.[63]

Ubbay Ibn Kaʿb, may God be pleased with him, related that the Emissary of God, God bless and cherish him, said the following: "Spread the good news to this Muslim community of glory, high rank, faith, and power on earth. But anyone who does a good deed for worldly gain, will have no share of it in the Hereafter." This is reported by Imām Aḥmad ibn Ḥanbal, al-Bayhaqī, Ibn Ḥibbān in his *Sound Traditions*, and al-Ḥākim, who said that its chain of 2.9

authorities was sound.[64] Ibn ʿAbbās, may God be satisfied with both him and his father, related that a man said, "O Emissary of God, when I stand on the Plain of ʿArafāt during the Hajj, I desire God, but I also want my standing there to be seen by others." The Emissary of God, God bless and cherish him, did not reply until the revelation came down: «Whoever hopes to meet his Lord, let him do righteous deeds and not associate anyone with worship of his Lord!»[65] Al-Ḥākim reports this and says that it is sound.[66]

2.10 It is related that the Prophet, God bless and cherish him, said as follows: "One who is hypocritical toward God for the sake of something other than God, has shunned God!" This is reported by al-Ṭabarānī. Abū Hurayrah, may God be pleased with him, related as follows: "I heard the Emissary of God, God bless and cherish him, say, 'Whoever is ostentatious with good deeds that he never intended or desired to do, is cursed in the heavens and on earth!'" Muʿādh ibn al-Jabal, may God be pleased with him, related from the Prophet, God bless and cherish him, as follows: "Any believer who is a hypocrite and cares for fame in this world below, will be denounced by God before the leaders of humanity on Judgment Day." Al-Ṭabarānī relates this with a good chain of authorities. Abū Hurayrah, may God be pleased with him, related that the Emissary of God, God bless and cherish him, said the following: "Whoever endears himself to the people with what they love, while confronting God with what is loathsome, will meet a wrathful God!" The Prophet, God bless and cherish him, also said, "Whoever does a good deed for worldly gain, his honor will be destroyed, memory of him will be effaced, and his name will be registered in Hell!" This is reported by al-Ṭabarānī in *The Great Collection* (*al-Kabīr*).

2.11 It is also related from the Prophet, may God bless and cherish him, that he said the following: "Seek refuge in God from the Pit of Sorrow!" They asked, "O Emissary of God, what is the Pit of Sorrow?" and he replied, "It is a ravine in Hell from which Hell itself seeks refuge four hundred times every day." Someone asked, "Who will enter it?" and he replied, "It is prepared for the hypocritical

Qur'an readers, and the most odious of Qur'an readers to God are those who visit tyrannical rulers." It is also related that the Emissary of God, may God bless and cherish him, said, "What I fear most for you is the lesser polytheism." "What is the lesser polytheism?" they asked, and he replied, "Hypocrisy. For mighty and glorious God will say when He rewards people for their actions, 'Go to those with whom you acted as hypocrites!'" Ibn Abī l-Dunyā and al-Bayhaqī report this. The Prophet, may God bless and cherish him, also said, "When God gathers together all the generations of people from the first to the last on the Day of Resurrection, about which there will be no doubt, a herald will proclaim, 'Whosoever in his actions took anyone as a partner with God, let him seek his reward from him, for God has no need of a partner!'" This is reported by al-Tirmidhī, Ibn Mājah, al-Bayhaqī, and Ibn Ḥibbān in his *Sound Traditions*. It is related that the Prophet, may God bless and cherish him, said, "God does not accept an action that has even the slightest bit of hypocrisy in it." Ibn Jarīr al-Ṭabarī reports this with an incomplete chain of authorities.

The Prophet, may God bless and cherish him, is reported to have 2.12
said as follows:

> On the Day of Resurrection, some people will be commanded to go toward the Garden, and they will draw near enough to smell its fragrance and gaze upon its palaces and what God has prepared there. Then they will be told that they are denied Paradise and will have absolutely no share of it. They will come away aggrieved, unlike those who returned before them, and they will say, "Our Lord, it would have been better for us had You thrown us into Hellfire before You showed us the reward that You have prepared for Your intimate friends!" and God will reply, "This is as I intended, for when you forsook Me, you wronged Me greatly. When you met people, you were humble and made a great show, unlike what you gave Me from your hearts. You feared people, but not Me; you honored people

> but not Me, and you left people your bequest, but left Me nothing. Today, I made you taste a grievous punishment through the reward forbidden to you!"

This is reported by al-Ṭabarānī in *The Great Collection* and by al-Bayhaqī.[67]

2.13 It is related that the Prophet, God bless and cherish him, said as follows: "On the Day of Resurrection sealed ledgers will be brought, and they will be opened before God the Exalted. God blessed and exalted will say, 'Reject this and accept this!' Then the angels will say, 'By Your glory, we see nothing but good deeds!' and mighty and glorious God will reply, 'This was not done for My sake, so I will not accept it! I accept only what was done for My sake.'" This is reported by al-Bazzār and al-Ṭabarānī.[68] The Prophet, God bless and cherish him, also said, "When God created the Garden of Eden, He created what no eye had ever seen, what no ear had ever heard, and what had never occurred to the mind of human beings. Then He said to the Garden, 'Speak!' and it said, '«The believers will prosper!»,'[69] and 'I am forbidden to every miser and hypocrite!'"[70]

2.14 Someone asked Yaḥyā ibn Muʿādh, may God be pleased with him, "When is a man sincere?" and he replied, "When his nature is that of a child." Someone asked Dhū l-Nūn al-Miṣrī, may God be pleased with him, "When does a believer know that he is one of God's elect?" and he answered, "When he gives up leisure and exerts himself, loving his decline in social status since praise and blame are equal in his sight." Fuḍayl ibn ʿIyāḍ said, "One who is sociable with people and distressed when alone is not safe from hypocrisy." Al-Anṭākī said,[71] "Self-adornment is a term with three meanings: adorning oneself with knowledge, adorning oneself with deeds, and adorning oneself by leaving behind all adornment, which is the most difficult and the most loved by God the Exalted." Ibrāhīm ibn Adham said, "One is not sincere in love of God if one loves fame."

2.15 ʿIkrimah said,[72] "By God, He rewards the servant based on his intention and not on his action. This is because the intention can have no hypocrisy in it." Wuhayb ibn al-Ward said, "If you want faith, then base it on three things: renunciation, piety, and sincerity. If you build on anything else, the building will collapse." Ibn Masʿūd said, "Salvation lies in two things: intention and shame, whereas destruction lies in two things: despair and pride." Al-Ḥasan al-Baṣrī said, "The people of Paradise will dwell in Paradise for eternity, and the people of Hellfire will dwell in Hellfire for eternity, based on their intentions." Abū Hurayrah, may God be pleased with him, said that it is written in the Torah as follows: "That which was intended for My sake, though it be little, is much, whereas that which was intended for other than Me, though it be much, is little." Fuḍayl ibn ʿIyāḍ, may God be pleased with him, said, "If a deed is proper but insincere, it is not accepted. If a deed is sincere but not proper, it is not accepted until it becomes both sincere and proper."

Ayyūb al-Sakhtiyānī, may God be pleased with him, said, "By God, a believer can never be sincere until he loves being oblivious to his rank." Fuḍayl ibn ʿIyāḍ, may God be pleased with him, said, "God always questions the righteous about their righteousness, including Jesus son of Mary, who wept in response. So imagine how it will be for the wretched hypocritical unbelievers!" Someone said to Dāwūd al-Ṭāʾī, "Your clothes are on inside out!" and he replied, "I dress this way for God, and I won't change it for another." ʿAlī ibn Abī Ṭālib, may God have mercy upon him, said, "The hypocrite has three characteristics: he is lazy when alone, but energetic around people; he will work harder if praised, and slack off when criticized." Abū Yaʿqūb al-Makfūf, may God be pleased with him, said, "The sincere person is one who hides his good deeds the way he hides his bad deeds."[73] Al-Ḥasan al-Baṣrī, may God be pleased with him, said, "A man was praised in the presence of the Prophet, God bless and cherish him, so the Prophet said, 'You have placed a great burden on him. Were he to hear your praise, he would never prosper again.'" 2.16

Shaqīq al-Balkhī, may God be pleased with him, said as follows: "You protect a good deed with three things: by believing the deed 2.17

is authorized by God, by undertaking the deed with God's blessing, and by seeking merit for the deed from God. Therefore, if you believe the authorization is from God, you will eliminate pride; if you undertake the deed with God's blessing, you will eliminate selfish desire; and if you seek merit from God, you will eliminate greed and hypocrisy, and the deed will be sincere."

2.18 Al-Ḥasan al-Baṣrī, may God be pleased with him, said, "The hypocrite wants to defeat God's decree; he is a man of evil who wants people to say that he is good. But he has fallen away from his Lord into the place of the wicked. There is no doubt that believers sense and know him for what he is. When a servant acts with hypocrisy, God the Exalted says, 'Look at My servant; he mocks Me!'"

2.19 Muʿādh ibn Jabal, may God be pleased with him, said, "An act requires four things to be safe from hypocrisy: knowledge before beginning it, proper intention at its start, patience during it, and sincerity at its conclusion." Someone asked Yaḥyā ibn Muʿādh al-Rāzī, may God be pleased with him, "When does the servant's life become sweet?" and he replied, "When he clings to the rank of servanthood." They said, "When does he cling to the rank of servanthood?" and he replied, "When he says sincerely in his heart to God, 'If You give to me, I will give thanks; if You forbid me, I will accept it; if You call me, I will answer; and if You leave Me, I will still serve.'"

2.20 Makḥūl[74] composed the following apt verses:

By seeking praise and glory with good deeds,
    you seek what can never be!
For God foils the hypocrite
    and thwarts the effort and toil.
«Whoever hopes to meet his Lord»[75]
    is sincere in deed out of fear of Him.
Heaven and Hell are in His hands,
    so be sincere, and He will grant you grace.

People own nothing, so don't go astray
trying so hard to win their sway!

Ruwaym said, "One who possesses sincerity does not desire compensation in this world or in the next, nor good fortune from either realm."[76] The master Abū l-Qāsim al-Qushayrī, may God be pleased with him, said the following: "Abū 'Alī al-Daqqāq said, 'Sincerity is to devote oneself to seek and obey the True Reality alone.' By obedience he means seeking nearness to God, mighty and glorious, and excluding all else, including showing off for others, seeking people's praise and loving it, or anything else, except drawing closer to God the Exalted."[77] Al-Qushayrī also said, "Sincerity is to devote oneself in worship to the True Reality, may He be glorified. Those whose deeds are tainted with hypocrisy are not sincere. It is said that sincerity is to be oblivious to others' opinions about you, and that sincerity is when you do not look for the place of distinction.[78] It is also said that sincerity is to regard yourself with a critical eye."[79] Al-Qushayrī said, "Sincere worship is to embrace the divine command with the utmost humility within one's self, heart, and spirit. Sincerity for one's self is to avoid being critical of others; sincerity for the heart is to be oblivious to others' opinions about you, and sincerity for the spirit is cleansing one's self of seeking to be distinguished."[80] This is true realization of true sincerity. 2.21

Abū Ya'qūb al-Sūsī related as follows: "Whenever people see sincerity in their own sincerity, their sincerity needs sincerity!"[81] We have composed verses on this subject:[82] 2.22

Whoever sees sincerity in their acts,
truly needs sincerity—that's a fact.
So beware lest one day you'll wonder why
you began or did some suspect act.

One of the Sufis said, "If you sincerely seek God, He will give you a mirror in which to consider everything." Fuḍayl ibn 'Iyāḍ, may God be pleased with him, said, "Neglecting to do a good deed in 2.23

order to please people is hypocrisy, whereas doing a good deed to please people is polytheism. Sincerity is that God protects you from both of those acts."[83] The Imām Abū 'Abd al-Raḥmān al-Sulamī, may God be pleased with him, related with an unbroken chain of authorities from al-Ḥasan al-Baṣrī, that al-Ḥasan said as follows:

> I asked Ḥudhayfah about sincerity, and he said, "I asked the Emissary of God, God bless and cherish him, about sincerity, and he said, 'I asked Gabriel, peace be upon him, about sincerity, and he said, "I asked the Lord of Might about sincerity, and He said, 'It is a secret of My mystery, which I place in the hearts of My servants whom I love.'"'"[84]

The judge Abū Bakr Ibn al-'Arabī in his *Prophetic Transmissions* (*al-Musalsalāt*), added the following to this: "No angel can attain the secret to record it, nor any devil to corrupt it."[85]

2.24 Know, may God show you mercy, that this is the true realization of sincerity, and the words of the Sufi folk, may God bless all of their inner hearts, point to the signs by which one can infer that someone who has them is sincere. Dhū l-Nūn al-Miṣrī, may God be pleased with him, said, "Sincerity has three signs: that praise and blame by the common people are of equal measure, that one is oblivious to good deeds while doing them, and that any reward is expected only in the Hereafter."[86] Ḥudhayfah al-Mar'ashī is related to have said, "Sincerity is when outward and inward actions match."[87] Similar is al-Qushayrī's statement: "The minimal requirement for truthfulness is that one's secret thoughts and public actions match." Sahl al-Tustarī, may God be pleased with him, related as follows: "The worshipper who flatters himself or others will not catch a whiff of truthfulness."[88] The sayings of the Sufi folk on this topic are innumerable, so we have recorded in this book what is sufficient for one given success by God. He is my sufficiency and «the best trustee»![89]

2.25 Know, may God show you mercy, that sincerity is a light dispelling the dark afflictions of concupiscence and Satan. Action is a wellspring, and hypocrisy is a pollutant, whereas sincerity is the secret from the mysteries of God that purifies this pollutant. By God, whoever piles up hypocrisy will have no share of the fragrance of the rose of acceptance! Sincerity is red sulfur. If an ounce of it were thrown on a ton of copper deeds, it would turn them into pure gold fit for a king.

The servant of God is never sincere in private without God's acceptance of him proclaimed in public. As for the hypocrite, God exposes him in this world by means of the spiritual insight of the Sufi masters, even before He exposes him in the Hereafter in public for all to witness. 2.26

There is no ascent to the high place of acceptance except on two wings: one is truthfulness, the other, sincerity. Hypocrisy is a pair of shears; if the wings are shorn by them, there will never be an ascent. Sincerity is water that causes the tiny seed of a good deed to grow, whereas hypocrisy is a cyclone of fire which, when it alights upon a field of deeds, consumes it! So choose for yourself what is sweetest! 2.27

God inspired me with the following verses exhorting sincerity:[90] 2.28

Be sincere, and with sincerity, be recorded as a believer
and leave hypocrisy, for that is polytheism.
In the world, many snares appear for you
devised by wretched Satan who stalks his prey!

Say to the one who is rich in the merchandise of deeds: "All this hypocrisy! It will bring you no profit, only toil. Do you really think that hypocritical acts can be a commodity? Wrong! Wrong! You have desired the impossible that will never be!" A house of good deeds raised up on the foundation of sincerity is sound forever, whereas that which is based on a foundation of hypocrisy is dilapidated, and the building will collapse. That is because the sincere person «lays the foundation for his building on constant vigilance for God and His approval,» whereas the hypocrite «lays his foundation on the brink of a precipice; it comes crashing down, and he is thrown along with it into the fire of Hell!»[91] 2.29

2.30 To the one who performs deeds in order to show off, say, "«Evil and good are not equal, though the abundance of evil delights you,»[92] as you mock Him and try to hide from Him who «knows the treacherous eyes and what the breasts conceal.»[93] Your arrow is wide of the mark!" How can the hypocrite's hypocrisy be hidden from Him «Who never misses an atom's weight»[94] on earth or in heaven? Woe to him who presents his good deeds to one who will do him no good, while he comes with shameful deeds before Him «Who has the command from the beginning and forever»![95] «They may hide from people, but they cannot hide from God who is always with them!»[96]

2.31 Sincerity has had an effect on beasts, so how much more on humans? Al-Damīrī reports in his *The Lives of Animals* (*Ḥayāt al-ḥayawān*) as follows:

> When God sent Adam, peace be upon him, down to Earth, a herd of gazelles came to him. So he prayed for them and stroked their backs. As a result, musk bags appeared on them. Then another herd asked them the cause of this musk, and they replied, "We visited Adam, peace be upon him, so he prayed for us, and stroked our backs." So the other herd went to him, and he prayed for them and stroked their backs, but they found no musk. Later, they said to the first herd: "We did as you did, but received no musk in return," and they replied: "We visited him for God's sake, but you did that for the sake of musk!"[97]

2.32 Praise Him who singled out for sincerity a distinguished group who made it their habit to conceal their mystical states and good deeds. Among them was one who dressed in fine garments and put a key in his sleeve when he went out among people to make others suppose that he owned a house, when, in fact, he lived in the mosques. Another one did not own even a robe, and when he was asked about that, he would say, "I have an allergy that prevents me from wearing a robe," but the real reason was his poverty. Another one when asked about his lineage and descent would say,

"My ancestors were shepherds and day laborers from the common folk." Another one gave alms with his right hand without his left hand knowing it. Among them was one who would leave a gathering when he was overcome by tears, and another one would disguise his tears by saying, "What a bad cold!" Among them was one who would lie down on his prayer rug to conceal his praying when someone asked to enter his place of prayer. Another one would cover up the copy of the Qur'an that he was reading if someone came near him. Another one would put healthy people's food next to him when he was ill to conceal his illness. Among them was one who would change weeping to laughter when he was overcome.

By God, these are the attributes of the sincere, the signs of 2.33
the truthful, the conduct of the gnostics, and the mark of those who profess oneness. May God place you and us among them through His grace and generosity. Indeed, He is the most merciful of those who give mercy! We have referred to these special folk in inspired verse:[98]

Honor a folk who use their concealment
as the door to be free from all evil.
They are the chosen, and when they suppress desire,
sincerity's sweet smell guides you to them.

This is the end of the second principle. Success comes from God 2.34
alone!

The Third Principle: Remembrance (*Dhikr*)

3.1 God the Exalted has said, «Therefore, remember Me, and I will remember you.»[99]

3.2 Al-Qushayrī, may God be pleased with him, writes:

> The way for the literalists is: «Therefore remember Me» with proper conduct, «and I will remember you» with miracles. But for the folk seeking mystical allusions, the way is: «So remember Me» by leaving everything else, «and I will remember you» by resurrecting you in My reality after your annihilation from yourselves. It is said, «Therefore remember Me,» content with Me without need of My grace and favors, «and I will remember you,» satisfied with you, without your actions. It is said, «Therefore remember Me» recalling My remembrance on your behalf. For were it not for My prior remembrance of you, you would have no subsequent remembrance.[100] It is said, «Remember Me» by severing attachments, «and I will remember you» with the attribute of realities, and it is said, «Remember Me» to whomever you meet, «and I will remember you» to whomever I address. It is said, «Remember Me» with self-abasement, «and I will remember you» with favor, and it is said, «Remember Me» with humility, «and I will remember you» with beneficence. It is said, «Remember Me» with the tongue, «and I will remember you» in the

> heart, and it is said, «Remember Me» in your hearts, «and I will remember you» with the realization of your desires. It is said, «Remember Me» at the door of service, «and I will remember you» with affirmation and sublime blessings on the carpet of proximity. It is said, «Remember Me» with a pure heart, «and I will remember you» with total kindness. It is said, «Remember Me» when you are happy, «and I will remember you» when you are in your graves, and it is said, «Remember Me» when you are in a state of well-being, «and I will remember you» on the Day of Resurrection when regret will be of no use. It is said, «Remember Me» with longing, «and I will remember you» with wonder.[101]

Al-Qushayrī mentions this in his *Subtleties of Mystical Allusions* (*Laṭā'if al-ishārāt*). He also says concerning this verse, "Be consumed in Our existence through your remembrance after your annihilation from yourselves."[102] 3.3

Al-Sulamī says, «Remember Me» with your utmost ability, and I will join your remembrance with My remembrance so that your remembrance will be realized.[103] 3.4

God inspired me with the following regarding this verse: 3.5

> «Remember Me» with sincerity, «and I will remember you» with favor. «Remember Me» fervently, «and I will remember you» with mystical vision. «Remember Me» truly, «and I will remember you» with kindness. «Remember Me» with exaltation, «and I will remember you» with honor. «Remember Me» in fear, «and I will remember you» with union. «Remember Me» by seeking refuge with Me, «and I will remember you» by fulfilling your hope. «Remember Me» through your annihilation in Me, «and I will remember you» by causing you to abide in Me. «Remember Me» with reverence, «and I will remember you» with proximity. «Remember Me» among humanity, «and I will remember you» with amity. «Remember Me» with total attention, «and I will

remember you» with a glorious epiphany. «Remember Me» in the heart, «and I will remember you» with nearness. «Remember Me» in the spirit, «and I will remember you» with spiritual inspirations. «Remember Me» in your inner hearts, «and I will remember you» with refulgent lights. «Give thanks to Me,»[104] for My benevolence to you when I say, «Remember Me, and I will remember you . . . and do not be ungrateful»[105] by forsaking remembrance.

3.6 The Exalted has said, «O you who believe, remember God often!»[106]

3.7 Al-Qushayrī writes,

The mystical allusion is "Love God" because, the Prophet, God bless and cherish him, said, "Someone who loves something, remembers it often." Therefore, he loves to say "God," and does not forget God after recollecting God. It is said that this means that you remember God in your hearts. The only remembrance that is possible to sustain permanently is the remembrance with the heart, for permanent remembrance with the tongue is impossible.[107]

3.8 The Exalted has said, «Those who believe and whose hearts are at peace with remembrance of God—truly, it is with remembrance of God that hearts are at peace!»[108]

3.9 Al-Qushayrī, may God be pleased with him, writes,

Some people have hearts that are at peace with remembrance of God, and they find their comfort in remembrance and attain their perfection by remembrance. The hearts of other folk are at peace through God's remembrance of them; He remembers them with His grace and establishes peace within their hearts in a manner specific to them. Someone said that when they remember that God has remembered them, their hearts become serene, their spirits rejoice, and their inner hearts find comfort. God the Exalted has said, «Truly, it is with remembrance of God that hearts are at peace!»[109] to underscore what kind of life is bestowed by God.[110]

Al-Sulamī, may God be pleased with him, writes, 3.10

> There are four types of hearts. The hearts of the common people find peace in remembrance of God by glorifying Him, praising Him, and lauding Him in consideration of the grace and well-being that He has bestowed. The hearts of the religious scholars find peace with the divine attributes, names, and qualities, so they ponder those manifestations over the ages. The hearts of the spiritual elite find peace in remembrance of God through their sincerity, their total dependence on Him, their gratitude, and fortitude, and so they rest in Him. As for those truly professing God's oneness, this is all incidental, for their hearts are not at peace in any mystical state![111]

Ibrāhīm al-Khawwāṣ, may God be pleased with him, has said, 3.11

> People are divided into two states. One type is always moving and running around and can be described as selfish, since his selfishness clearly dominates. As the Exalted has said, «The human being is hasty.»[112] The other type remains tranquil and can be described as being with the True Reality, since the True Reality clearly dominates his tranquility. God the Exalted has said, «Truly it is with remembrance of God that hearts are at peace!»[113]

Al-Ḥusayn said,[114] "One who, in his pre-eternal state, is remembered favorably by the True Reality is at peace with Him for eternity." Al-Nahrajūrī said, "The hearts of the saints are loci for spiritual insights, so the saints are never agitated or disquieted. Rather, the saints are tranquil out of fear that He might suddenly bring spiritual insights to the heart while they are in an unseemly state."[115] 3.12

The Exalted has said, «Indeed, the remembrance of God is greater!»[116] Al-Qushayrī writes, 3.13

«God's remembrance is greater» than the remembrance by created things because His remembrance is eternal, whereas the remembrance by created things is temporal. It is said that the worshipper's remembrance of God is greater than the worshipper's remembrance of other things because the remembrance of Him is an act of obedience, whereas remembrance of any other thing is not.[117] It is said that «the remembrance of God is greater» when it is free of seeking any benefit in exchange, whether out of fear of punishment or in hope of reward. It is said that «God's remembrance is greater» than your remembrance of yourselves.[118] It is said that His remembrance of you with good fortune is better than your remembrance of Him in worship. «Remembrance of God is so great» that no one knows its power, and so great that no other remembrance can compare. Some say that «remembrance of God is so great» that it allows no melancholy to abide with it and that «remembrance of God is so great» that it leaves no sign or trace of the worshipper to abide with it.[119] It is said that «remembrance of God is so great» that lovers cannot live without it.[120]

3.14 There are other verses on remembrance, and were it not for fear of being long-winded, I would have cited most of them. But this should suffice one whom God has blessed with success.

3.15 As for prophetic traditions on remembrance, they are nearly countless, including one related by Abū Hurayrah, may God be pleased with him, as follows: "The Emissary of God, God bless and cherish him, said, 'Those devoted to religion alone lead the way.' They asked, 'Who are these devoted ones, O Emissary of God?' He said, 'Those devoted to the remembrance of God. Remembrance removes the burdens of their sin, so on the Day of Resurrection they will come forward unladen.'" This is reported by al-Tirmidhī, who says it is a good hadith, though with only a single chain of transmission. Muslim reports something similar, though he exchanged "those who remember God often" for "those devoted."

ʿAbd Allāh ibn Busr, may God be pleased with him, related as follows: "A man said, 'O Emissary of God, the different paths of Islam are many. Teach me something to cling to,' and the Prophet replied, 'Keep your tongue moist with the remembrance of God the Exalted!'" This is reported by al-Tirmidhī, who also relates from Abū Saʿīd al-Khudrī, may God be satisfied with him, as follows: "The Prophet, God bless and cherish him, was asked, 'Which type of worshipper is preferred by God on the Day of Resurrection?' He replied, 'Those who remember God often.' 'O Emissary of God,' I said, 'more than being a holy warrior fighting in the path of God?' and he said, 'Were one to wield his sword among the infidels and polytheists until his sword was broken and he was dyed with blood, those who remember God would still be preferable to him!'" Abū l-Dardāʾ, may God be pleased with him, related that the Prophet, God bless and cherish him, said, "Shall I tell you what is your best and purest act before your Lord, the deed that raises you highest, one greater than spending gold and silver in charity and better than meeting and fighting your enemies?" "Yes, of course, O Emissary of God!" everyone replied, and he said, "Remembrance of God the Exalted!" Al-Tirmidhī and al-Bayhaqī report this. 3.16

Ibn ʿUmar, may God be pleased with both him and his father, related that the Prophet, God bless and cherish him, said, "Speak little, except in remembering God the Exalted. Indeed, excessive talk without the remembrance of God leads to a hardening of the heart. Surely, those farthest from God are the hard-hearted." Al-Tirmidhī reports this. The Prophet, God bless and cherish him, is also reported to have said, "Comparing one who remembers God to one who does not remember God is like comparing the living to the dead." Al-Bukhārī relates this from Abū Mūsā al-Ashʿarī. 3.17

Muʿādh ibn Anas, may God be pleased with him, related that the Emissary of God, God bless and cherish him, said, "God, may His remembrance be glorified, has said, 'A worshipper never remembers Me in his heart without Me remembering him within an assembly of My angels, and he never remembers Me in an assembly without Me 3.18

remembering him in the highest gathering.'" Al-Ṭabarānī reports this. Ibn 'Abbās, may God be pleased with both him and his father, related that the Prophet, God bless and cherish him, said, "God, the Glorious and Exalted, has said, 'O son of Adam, if you remember Me when alone, I will remember you likewise, and if you remember Me in an assembly, I will remember you in an assembly better than the one where I am remembered.'" Al-Bazzār reports this. Abū Hurayrah, may God be pleased with him, related that the Prophet, God bless and cherish him, said, "Truly God, the Glorious and Exalted, has said, 'I am with My servant when he thinks of Me, and I am with him when he remembers Me, and when I am on his lips.'" This is reported by Ibn Mājah, as quoted here, and by Ibn Ḥibbān in his *Sound Traditions*.

3.19 Abū Sa'īd al-Khudrī, may God be pleased with him, related that the Prophet, God bless and cherish him, said, "Constantly mention God such that people will say, 'You're possessed!'" This was related by Imām Aḥmad ibn Ḥanbal, Abū Ya'lā, Ibn Ḥibbān in his *Sound Traditions*, and al-Ḥākim, who said that the chain of authorities was sound. In another tradition reported by al-Ṭabarānī, the Prophet said, "Remember to mention God so often that the hypocrites will say that you are being ostentatious." Anas, may God be pleased with him, related from the Prophet, may God bless and cherish him, as follows: "Satan has placed his snout on the heart of every person; if one remembers God, Satan withdraws, but if one forgets God, Satan devours his heart!" Ibn Abī l-Dunyā reports this, as do Abū Ya'lā, and al-Bayhaqī. (The "snout" is a muzzle.)

3.20 Abū l-Mukhāriq, may God be pleased with him, related that the Prophet, may God bless and cherish him, said, "When God took me on the Night Journey, I passed a man hidden in the light of God's throne. I asked if he was an angel, and was told no. I asked if he was a prophet, and was told no. So I asked who he was, and was told that he was a man whose tongue was always moist with the remembrance of God when he lived in this world below, whose heart was always attached to mosques, and who had never said an unkind word to his parents." Ibn Abī l-Dunyā reports this.

Abū Hurayrah, may God be pleased with him, related that the Emissary of God, God bless and cherish him, said, "The one who does not remember God often is devoid of faith." This is reported by al-Ṭabarānī in his *Shorter Work* (*al-Ṣaghīr*) and in his *Middle Work* (*al-Awsaṭ*). Abū Hurayrah, may God be pleased with him, also relates that the Prophet, God bless and cherish him, said that God the Exalted will say, "O son of Adam, when you remember Me, you thank Me, but when you forget Me, you are ungrateful to Me!" Al-Ṭabarānī reports this in his *Middle Work*. Ibn ʿUmar, may God be pleased with both him and his father, related that the Emissary of God, God bless and cherish him, said, "When remembrance of Me distracts a worshipper from making a request of Me, I give him something better than I give to those who petition Me." Al-Ṭabarānī reports this in his *Book of Prayer* (*Kitāb al-Duʿāʾ*). 3.21

Anas, may God be pleased with him, related that the Prophet, God bless and cherish him, said, "If you pass by the meadows of the Garden, graze there." "What are the meadows of the Garden, O Apostle of God?" they asked, and he replied, "The chanting circles of recollection." This is reported by al-Tirmidhī. Ibn ʿUmar, may God be pleased with both him and his father, reports as follows, "I said, 'O, Apostle of God, what is the prize to be gained from recollection sessions?' and he replied, 'The prize to be gained from recollection sessions is the Garden.'" Imām Aḥmad reports this with a good chain of authorities. 3.22

Muʿāwiyah, may God be pleased with him, related as follows: 3.23

> The Prophet, God bless and cherish him, confronted a circle of his companions and said, "What brought you together?" They replied, "We sat together to remember God and to praise Him for His guidance and blessings upon us with Islam." The Prophet said, "By God, did nothing bring you together but that?" "By God, nothing

> brought us together but that!" they answered. "I was about to make you swear an oath," he replied, "as I was suspicious of you, but Gabriel, peace be upon him, came to me and informed me that God, mighty and glorious, boasts about you among His angels!"

Muslim reports this and the following.

3.24 Abū Saʿīd al-Khudrī and Abū Hurayrah, may God be pleased with both of them, also related that they heard the Emissary of God, God bless and cherish him, say, "No people sit down to remember God the Exalted without the angels enfolding them; peace of mind descends upon them, mercy enwraps them, and God mentions them to those who are with Him." Anas, may God be pleased with him, also related, "No folk gather to recollect God for His sake alone, without a herald calling out to them from heaven, saying: 'Arise, you have been forgiven! Your sins have been exchanged for good deeds!'" Imām Aḥmad reports this. Anas also related that the Prophet, God bless and cherish him, said, "Indeed, God has wandering hosts of angels who seek out circles of recollection, and enfold them when they come upon them. Then the angels send forth their advance guard to the Lord of Power, blessed and exalted, in heaven above, saying: 'Our Lord! We came upon a group of Your worshippers glorifying Your favors, reciting from Your book, praying for their prophet Muḥammad, God bless and cherish him, and beseeching You for their reward in the Hereafter.' Then God, blessed and exalted, says: 'Wrap them in My mercy, for they are the close companions in whose company no companion is unhappy!'" Al-Bazzār reports this.

3.25 It is related that the Prophet, God bless and cherish him, said, "To the right of the Throne—and both of its sides are the right side—are men, neither prophets nor martyrs, whose bright faces are blessed with the vision of those who gaze upon God. The prophets and the martyrs envy them for their place and proximity with God, mighty and glorious." The Prophet was asked, "O Emissary of God, who are they?" and he replied, "They are the cream of the crop from all the tribes, who gather together to remember God. They select the sweetest speech just as someone eating dates will select the sweetest ones!" Al-Ṭabarānī reports this. It means that they did not gather together due to kinship or lineage or acquaintance; rather, they gathered together to remember God the Exalted, and nothing else.

Know, may God show you mercy, that the hadiths on the benefit of remembrance are innumerable, but what I have related here suffices those granted success by God. 3.26

There are numerous statements on this topic by the pious forebears among the companions, their followers, and the favored saints. These include the statement by Muʿādh ibn Jabal, may God be pleased with him, who said, "No deed is more efficacious in saving one from God's punishment than the remembrance of God." When he was asked, "Not even jihad in the way of God?" he replied, "Not even jihad. For God has said, «Indeed, remembrance of God is greater!»"[121] Al-Ḥasan al-Baṣrī said, "Were God to impose upon us the remembrance of Him in such and such a land, so that He might remember us, then it would be incumbent on us to go to that land and remember Him, as a way for Him to remember us. So just imagine, we are at home or attending a gathering or on the road, and we remember Him, then He remembers us. It is just as He has said: «Remember Me, and I will remember you!»"[122] Al-Fuḍayl ibn ʿIyāḍ, may God be pleased with him, said, "Remembering people is a disease; remembering God is a cure." 3.27

Ibrāhīm ibn Adham, may God be pleased with him, once saw a man speaking about worldly things, so he went up to him and said, "Are you hoping your words will bring you heavenly reward?" "No," he replied, and Ibrāhīm said, "Will they protect you from divine punishment?" "No," he replied, and Ibrāhīm said, "Then don't use affected language with no hope of reward or means of protection against punishment. Instead, you should remember God." Another said as follows: "I have heard that every person will leave this world parched with thirst, except those who remember God." Another 3.28

said, "There is no happier day in my life than when I go out for some reason, and the remembrance of God occurs to me!" Mālik ibn Dīnār said, "Nothing delights those who savor spiritual delights like the remembrance of God." Fuḍayl once said, "One who remembers God is happy, rich, and safe; he is happy with remembrance, rich in heavenly reward, and safe from sin."

3.29 Wuhayb ibn al-Ward said, "Whenever people gather together as a group, the one closest to God is the one who begins by remembering God, while the one farthest from God begins by remembering other people." Thābit al-Bunānī said, "I certainly know when my Lord remembers me." Some people were taken aback by this and said, "You know that?" "Yes," he replied, and they asked, "How?" So he said, "When I remember Him, He remembers me!" Muʿādh ibn Jabal said, "The people of Paradise are never distressed about anything except for the time they are not spending in the remembrance of God the Exalted." Anas ibn Mālik, may God be pleased with him, said, "Every morning and evening the valleys of the earth shout to one another, 'O neighbor, has anyone passed you today remembering God and rejoicing in Him?'" Al-Ḥasan al-Baṣrī said, "Burnish these hearts with the remembrance of God, for they are quick to sin!"

3.30 Know, may God show you mercy, that the enlightened ones have many mystical sayings about true remembrance. Al-Kalābādhī, may God show him mercy, said, "True remembrance is that you forget everything save the One remembered in the remembrance, in accordance with the statement of God the Exalted, «Remember your Lord when you forget.»[123] This means that when you forget everything but God, you have then remembered God."[124] May God show you mercy as you reflect on the awesomeness of this statement and how true it is, for it is indeed the true certainty regarding the true remembrance.

3.31 Even more awesome is the following statement by Dhū l-Nūn al-Miṣrī, may God be pleased with him: "One who truly remembers God, forgets everything in the midst of his remembrance. God protects him from everything and is his compensation for everything."

When he was asked about remembrance, he replied, "It is the absence of the one who remembers in the remembrance." Then, he recited,

> I remember You again and again, not because I forgot You,
> but because recollection flows from my tongue![125]

3.32 One of the gnostics said, "Remembrance drives away heedlessness. So if heedlessness disappears, you are remembering, even if you are silent." Even loftier than this statement is the following by one of the realized masters: "When a person remembers within his inner heart, the tongue's recollection may disturb him, for he is immersed in contemplation and in the presence, absent from all but the One remembered." The following is ascribed to al-Junayd:

> I remembered You without forgetting you for a moment,
> and the easiest recollection is with the tongue.[126]

3.33 Al-Qushayrī said, "Remembrance is the immersion of the one remembering in contemplation of the One remembered, followed by his annihilation in the contemplation of the One remembered such that no trace is left in you to remember. Then people will say, 'Once, so-and-so used to exist!'"[127] Sumnūn said, "True remembrance is to forget everything except the One being remembered due to one's immersion in Him, so one is remembering Him all the time." Then he recited,

> I remember You again and again, not because I forgot You,
> but because recollection flows from my tongue!

3.34 One of the Sufis said, "How can one remember the True Reality with mere created intellects and natural imaginations? How can one remember in time the One who was before time by His very nature, since the True Reality preceded everything remembered except Himself?" Another said, "The perfect remembrance is that you constantly contemplate in your remembrance of Him, the remembrance of you by the One remembered." Al-Wāsiṭī said,

"True remembrance is the abandonment of remembrance and forgetting it while standing with the One remembered."

3.35 One of the Sufis said,

> Remembrance has a beginning, which is true attention. It has a middle, which is a guiding light. It has an end, which is a transcendent state. It has a root, which is purity; a branch, which is fidelity; a condition, which is presence; a field, which is righteous deeds; and a special feature, which is clear victory.

3.36 Abū Saʿīd al-Kharrāz said,

> When God the Exalted wants to befriend a worshipper, He opens the door of remembrance for him, and if the worshipper finds remembrance pleasant, God then opens the door of nearness for him. Then He raises him up to the intimate gatherings and seats him on the throne of oneness. There, God raises the veils from him and brings him into the incomparable abode, and reveals to him His glory and splendor. When the worshipper beholds the glory and splendor, he abides without individual being, for he will be annihilated from himself, abiding with his Lord.[128]

3.37 Another Sufi said, "Remembrance is the sinners' antidote and the exile's intimacy. It is a treasure for those who depend on God alone, nourishment for those with certainty, adornment for the seekers, and the public square of the gnostics." When al-Wāsiṭī was asked about remembrance, he replied, "It is leaving the public square of heedlessness, and entering the vast space of contemplation due to desire's dominance and love's intensity!"[129] Abū Bakr al-Kattānī said, "Were it not that recollection of Him was required of me as a religious duty, I could not mention Him out of awe for Him. How can one like me recollect Him without washing out his mouth a thousand times as a required penance, so great is His recollection and so awesome His name!"[130]

Abū Yazīd al-Bisṭāmī was asked, "What is the meaning of remembrance?" and he replied, "That the one remembering does not waver in contemplation and does not neglect his duty to remain focused on the Presence." One of the Sufis said, "One who does not taste the sweetness of being away from people, will never savor the intimacy of remembrance." Abū ʿUthmān al-Ḥīrī said, "Remember God with a recollection in which your tongues and hearts unite." He was told, "We remember God, but we do not find sweetness in our hearts," and he replied, "Then praise God the Exalted for adorning your tongue with obedience, and seek from Him the same good fortune for your hearts."[131] Abū l-Ḥusayn al-Dīnawārī said, "The most suitable remembrance is to forget all but Him. The end of remembrance is when the one remembering disappears in the remembrance from the remembrance and is immersed in the One remembered without returning to the stage of remembrance. This state is the annihilation of annihilation." 3.38

One of the Sufis recited the following: 3.39

Remembrance of the Lord seized my heart,
  and from my desire, I was drawn to Him.
Perhaps a glance to the heart will cure my state,
  for, wretched and in shame, I cling to Him.
When my ear hears mention of You,
  I am gripped with a passion, rending my heart.
It dies at Your mention, but lives by Your grace,
  while it grows in love from desire.

Know that the best recollection is the profession of oneness, which is to say, «There is no deity but God!»[132] Al-Tirmidhī and Ibn Mājah report this on the authority of Jābir ibn ʿAbd Allāh, may God be pleased with both him and his father, who said, "The Emissary of God, God bless and cherish him, said, 'The best recollection is: There is no deity but God!'" If you wish to be certain of this, know that the hadiths on the nobility and excellence of this profession 3.40

of faith are innumerable. Were it not for fear of deviating from the purpose of this book, I would cite some of them. Success comes from God alone!

3.41 Al-Qushayrī, may God be pleased with him, writes:

> The person who is truly certain regarding this statement—that is: «There is no deity but God»[133]—needs nothing from anyone but Him, and sees nothing but Him. He holds true to Him with exclusive devotion, perpetually alone in His existence. Thus, he hears only God through God, and he bears witness only to God; he does not draw near anything but God, and he is not occupied with anything but God. He is effaced from everything but God, and so has no complaint or claim, and places no stock in anything else. For when the True Reality takes full control of a servant, then absolutely no portion of him can remain. In fact, the true realization of «There is no deity but God» requires the complete annihilation of all traces of him![134]

3.42 Al-Qushayrī also writes regarding the exalted saying «*Alif lam mīm*. God, there is no deity but Him!»[135] as follows:

> God is never distracted from you, never forgetful, so you are never apart from Him. He keeps watch over your inner heart in all of your states; if you are in seclusion, He is watching you, and if you are among people, He is watching you. Whatever your state, He is your love![136]

3.43 Regarding the exalted saying «God bears witness,»[137] al-Qushayrī writes as follows:

> That is, God knows, God informs, and God decrees that «there is no deity but Him.»[138] This is the testimony of the True Reality to the True Reality that He is the True Reality and, so, the first to bear witness to God was God. For He bore witness in His eternity with His words, statement, and eternal address, and He made known His unique existence,

> His eternal being, His true self, His everlasting essence, His endless awe, and His eternal beauty. He, may He be glorified, bore witness to the perfection of His power and the awesomeness of His might when there was no unbelief or ignorance, when no creature had intellect or gnosis, when there was no covenant or infidelity, no temporality or difference, no atheism or polytheism, no understanding or falsehood, no sky or space, no light or darkness, no opposite principles, and no divisions of time.[139]

Regarding the exalted saying «Know, there is no deity but God,»[140] al-Qushayrī writes as follows: 3.44

> God ordered exclusive devotion to Him by blocking out all thought of creation, followed by blocking out all thought of oneself in exclusive devotion to Him. Therefore, if the worshipper utters this phrase out of habit, heedless of its truth, then he is oblivious, and the saying will be of little worth. Similarly, if the worshipper is amazed by something and utters this phrase, it will have no value. But if the worshipper says it with sincerity, remembering its meaning and realizing its truth, then he is sincere. However, if the worshipper says it while thinking of himself, then he is in exile, for the Sufis regard this as hidden polytheism. Yet, if the worshipper says it correctly, then that is true sincerity. The worshipper first learns of his Lord through evidence and proof, and so his self-awareness is acquired; this is a fundamental principle upon which all deductive knowledge is based. Then, his capacity for knowledge increases through further demonstrations and proofs. However, his self-awareness will decline when the remembrance of God overwhelms Him. If this ultimately leads to the mystical state of contemplation, and the power of truth seizes him, then his knowledge in that state will be immediate. His perception of himself will lessen as will discursive reason, and he will become unaware, forgetful of himself. Some

> say that staring at the ocean may overwhelm a person from thinking of himself, and if he then falls into the ocean, he will have no sensation other than of drowning in it.[141]

3.45 Ibn Manṣūr said, "Saying 'There is no deity but God' necessitates two things: dissociating God's lordship from any cause, and declaring the True Reality to be beyond comprehension." One of the Sufis said, "Saying 'There is no deity but God,' necessitates four qualities in one who says it: faith, glorification of God, pleasantness, and reverence. He who lacks faith is a hypocrite, and he who fails to praise is a fake. He who is not pleasant is a show-off, and he who lacks reverence is a profligate." Another said, "The one who says it must quit complaining in times of trouble, stop being disobedient in good times, and not be heedless in thought." Al-Shiblī was told, "Say, 'There is no god but God,'" and he replied, "I will say 'God,' but I won't offend Him with a denial of Him!" Another said, "One who says it with desire, fear, craving, or a demand in his heart is a polytheist."

3.46 I will conclude discussion of this principle with a sublime account of its meaning:

> Al-Shiblī was asked, "Why do you say 'God' but not 'There is no deity'?" and he replied, "Because Abū Bakr al-Ṣiddīq gave away all his wealth, leaving nothing behind. In a simple garment, he came before the Emissary of God, God bless and cherish him, who said to him, 'What have you left for your family?' He replied, 'God the Exalted! That is why I say "God"!'" The questioner then said to al-Shiblī, "Tell me something better," and al-Shiblī said, "I am ashamed to say a negative word in His presence!" The questioner said, "Tell me something better," so al-Shiblī said, "I am afraid that I will die while saying the denial 'There is no deity' without arriving at the affirmation 'but God'!" The questioner insisted, "Tell me something better," to which al-Shiblī replied, "God the Exalted said to His Emissary, «Say 'God,' then leave them to go round and round in their

speculation!»"[142] At that point, the young man stood up and let out a scream, and al-Shiblī exclaimed, "God!" The youth screamed again, and al-Shiblī exclaimed, "God!" Then he screamed a third time and died. The youth's relatives grabbed al-Shiblī and accused him of murder, and they went to the caliph and pressed their charge. The caliph said to al-Shiblī, "What is your plea?" and al-Shiblī answered, "He was a spirit who loved and longed, who sensed and shouted, who was called and heard, who knew and responded. What is my sin in this?" So the caliph proclaimed, "Release him!"

Know, may God show you mercy, that remembrance is one of the signs of love. The greatest beloved, the prophet Muḥammad, may God bless and cherish him, said, "The one who loves something, remembers it often." So what a privilege and honor for the one who remembers, that he is remembered by the True Reality, who has made a promise that He will never break: «Remember Me, and I will remember you!»[143] 3.47

Remembrance, then, is the means to attain what is hoped for. When God the Exalted wants to befriend one of His worshippers, He helps him to remember Him constantly until he is submerged in Him. When he is submerged in Him, the banners of sainthood are unfurled, the honor of grace arrives, and the most excellent of receptions is made ready. The ascension to union will occur, the door of nearness will be opened, and he will be ushered into the presence of vision, and seated on the carpet of intimacy. He will be attired in the robe of approval, crowned with the crown of election, presented with the gifts of distinction, and addressed with the kind words of the divine presence. The drink of fealty will come round in the cup of sincerity, and he will drink and be quenched. He will behold and be delighted when the Cupbearer appears to him with the grace of beauty and the beauty of perfection. As someone has said, 3.48

What happened, happened, but I will never tell,
so assume the best, and do not ask![144]

Thus, the ascending sun of the True Reality erases the shadow of difference, as the voice of glory chants the majestic declaration of true divine oneness: «Say, "He is God, one!"»[145] «Thus, protection belongs to God, the True Reality, and He is the best reward, and the best of ends!»[146]

3.49 God inspired me with the following verses:

I recalled You with a recollection that began from You,
so I disappeared from memory, immersed in You.
For nothing remained of me to speak save You
to speak for me from within and without!

3.50 That is true remembrance, leading to the goal after you have experienced poverty, tasted humility, embraced submission, and achieved constant tranquility; you must scatter tears, be sincere in repentance and true in sincerity. In everything, you must turn to God and abstain from all else, ridding yourself of any claims, continuously turning toward the One recalled, may He be glorified, turning to Him, facing Him, and seeking His help for the true remembrance of Him. Then your remembrance will be by Him and to Him, such that you will disappear from the remembrance into the One recalled, then from the One recalled, into the disappearance of obliteration and annihilation. This will lead you to abide in the presence of the One you remembered, in an everlasting life in Eden with Him and with the comfort of His nearness, in a life of felicity with whatever you desire of vision, union, and benevolence, and with the invitation «They will have whatever they desire there, and We have still more!».[147]

3.51 God inspired me with the following poem on remembrance:

The heart is a meadow revived by the water of remembrance,
and the heart is drunk there when He quenches it.
The trees of inspiration blossom from the emanation of grace,
with a bloom yielding fruit when He reveals Himself.

So remember Him without wants or desires;
  be sincere and humbly hold to recollection's rules,
And persist in remembrance till you disappear from you in God,
  leading you, in the end, to obliteration in Him.
In that loss, immortality will come to you with Him
  in whom you passed away, so live with Him, by Him, in Him
In a pleasant life, forever, in the gardens of fulfillment,
  quenched by a cup whose Bearer is the heart's love.
This is the life, Saʿd, which only the heart holds
  with all that it desires![148]

Regarding the proper conduct for remembrance, God inspired the following couplet:[149] 3.52

All of recollection's rules, I will tell you,
  so listen, remember, and choose success:
repentance, humility, ecstasy, friendship, and fear,
  truth, presence, purity, fidelity, and flowing tears.

With this, the third principle is completed. Success comes from God alone! 3.53

The Fourth Principle: Love (*Maḥabbah*)

4.1 God the Exalted has said, «Say, "If you love God, then follow me, and God will love you!"»[150]

4.2.1 Al-Qushayrī writes:

> Love requires the total effacement of yourself such that you are consumed in your beloved. A Sufi said,[151]
>
> There is no love till eyes flow with tears,
> and you're struck dumb and can't answer the caller![152]
>
> This is the difference between the beloved and the dear friend. The dear friend has said, «"He who follows me is of me,"»[153] whereas the beloved has said, «Say, "If you love God, then follow me, and God will love you!"»[154] The follower of the dear friend attains favor, but the follower of the beloved becomes the beloved of the True Reality, and thereby attains proximity to Him and a mystical state. God has dashed the hopes of all humanity that He would give Himself to anyone but their exemplar, the master of all who came before him and of those who come after, the prophet Muḥammad, may God bless and cherish him![155]
>
> 4.2.2 It is said that in this verse of the Qur'an just mentioned is an indication that love is not an effect, nor is it procured by obedience or by being free of evil, because He said,

«God loves you and forgives your sins.»[156] The "and" here, denotes a sequence so that it is clear that love is prior to forgiveness: first, He loves them; then they love Him, and then He forgives them, as they ask His pardon. Love thus necessitates forgiveness, because to forgive necessitates love.[157]

It is said that the term "love" (*maḥabbah*) indicates the purity of states, as in the expression "the dew (*ḥabab*) of teeth," meaning they are pure white. It is also said that love requires unmoving devotion to the cherished presence of the beloved in the inner heart; thus one says, "The camel knelt (*aḥabba*) and would not move" when it knelt down, and would not budge even when whipped.[158] Just so, the lover keeps nothing back from his beloved in either his heart or body.[159] 4.2.3

Al-Qushayrī also writes in *Commentary on the Divine Names* (*Sharḥ asmāʾ Allāh al-ḥusnā*) regarding the name "The Fashioner" (*al-muṣawwir*) as follows:[160] 4.3

It has been related in lore and tradition that God created six hundred wings for Gabriel, prayers and peace upon him—inlaid with sapphires, pearls, and golden bells, and suffused with musk. Each bell has a sublime sound and tone, unlike any other. When the archangel Israfel begins to sing the praise of God, he interrupts the angelic choir due to the sublime sound and pleasant tone. Similarly, the light of the divine throne, were it to appear, would outshine the light of the sun to the same degree that the sun outshines a lamp. There are other examples of created things, yet God, may He be praised, never said of such things that they were in the best of forms, nor did He say to any of them, "Indeed, I created you «of the best stature.»"[161] However, He said that to this human being created «from an extract of clay.»[162] But enough of things in nature. Let us move on to the exalted saying «He loves them, and they love Him.»[163] Did He ever say something comparable to an attending angel or to some created thing shaped in a beautiful form?

> Never! This was said of the children of Adam, exclusively. It was bestowed upon them above all others as a grace from God, as a favor and a benefit with which He graced them in an act of kindness and mercy.

4.4 Regarding His saying, may He be praised, «O you who believe, those of you who turn away from their religion, God will replace them with a folk whom He loves and who love Him,»[164] al-Qushayrī writes as follows:

> He describes the one who does not turn away from religion as loved by Him, may He be praised, and so, in turn, that worshipper loves Him. In this verse is an awesome and propitious tiding for believers! It has been said that if He had not loved them, then, certainly, they could never have loved Him, and that had He not spoken of love, how, then, could clay ever have had the courage to mention love? God then adds to the description of the lovers, saying they are «humble before the believers,»[165] since they sacrifice their hearts for the Beloved without animosity, and sacrifice their spirits to protect the Beloved, without holding back even a tiny sliver for their own comfort. He then says of them, «They strive in the path of God, and they do not fear the blamer's blame,»[166] since they strive within themselves to carry out all religious injunctions, strive in their hearts to curb wishes and desires, strive in their spirits to eliminate attachments, and strive in their inner hearts to stand straight and firm in contemplation at all times. He then says, «They do not fear the blamer's blame,»[167] since they pay no attention to the company of friends, nor seek personal fortune, nor feel the burden of fate or fortune, while never swerving from the path of fidelity. God, may He be praised, makes clear that this is not something from them, but rather something due to Him, as He says, «That is the grace of God, which He gives to whom He wills, for God is ever present, all knowing!»[168] Here end the words of al-Qushayrī.

Al-Wāsiṭī said of this verse: "Just as He loves them in His essence, so they love His essence. For the pronominal suffix 'Him' refers to the essence, free of qualities and attributes."[169] Al-Sulamī writes, "I heard al-Sulāmī say, 'Due to the grace of His love for them, they love Him, and due to the grace of His remembrance of them, they remember Him.'" Al-Wāsiṭī said, "Their love for Him emerges from His mention of His love for them. As the Exalted has said, «He loves them, so they love Him.»[170] How else could spiritual attributes arise from eternal, everlasting attributes?" Abū ʿUthmān al-Ḥīrī said regarding this verse, "He mentions His love for them and their love for Him. Then, He describes them, in His love for them, as «humble before believers.»[171] Humility, therefore, is clearly a quality of love. This is the opposite of arrogance, which is born of ignorance and leads to pain and woe, whereas humility is born of knowledge." Al-Junayd said, "One who asserts his love for God without the precondition of God's love of him—his claim is vain, until God first confirms His love for him. God has said, «God will replace them with a people whom He loves and who love Him.»"[172] 4.5

There is a hadith related by al-Bukhārī and Muslim on the authority of Anas, may God be pleased with him, who quoted the Prophet as saying, "Whoever possesses three qualities, will find the sweetness of faith: that he loves God and His Emissary more than anything else; that he loves another worshipper only for the love of God; and that he loathes a return to unbelief after God has saved him from it, as much as one loathes being thrown into fire."[173] 4.6

Al-ʿIrbāḍ ibn Sāriyah, may God be satisfied with him, related, "The Emissary of God, God bless and cherish him, used to pray saying, 'O God, make my love of You stronger than my love of myself, than of my hearing and sight, than of my family and all that I possess, and than even of fresh water itself!'"[174] Also related about the Prophet, may God bless and cherish him, "A man asked him about the Final Hour, and he replied, 'What have you prepared for it?' He said, 'I have not prepared with many prayers or much fasting, but I truly love God and His Emissary!' The Emissary of God, 4.7

may God bless and cherish him, replied, 'Each person will be made to stand on Judgment Day with those he loves!'" Anas said, "Beside Islam itself, I have never seen Muslims so delighted with anything as that prospect."

4.8 'Umar ibn al-Khaṭṭāb, may God be satisfied with him, related, "The Prophet, may God bless and cherish him, looked approvingly on Muṣ'ab ibn 'Umayr, may God be satisfied with him, who was wearing only a ram's fleece. The Prophet, God bless and cherish him, said, 'Look at this man whose heart God has illuminated. I once saw him with his parents, who fed him the finest food and drink, but love of God and His Emissary called him to what you are witnessing.'"[175]

4.9 The Prophet, may God bless and cherish him, related that God has said, "Whoever treats a friend of mine as an enemy has declared war on Me! My worshipper draws near to Me by nothing I love more than the religious obligations I have imposed upon him. Then, he continues to draw near Me by acts of willing devotion until I love him, and when I love him, I become his hearing, his sight, his tongue, his heart, his mind, his hand, and his support!"[176] Al-Bukhārī relates this. This honorable tradition alone is sufficient regarding the honor and glory given to the worshipper whom God has befriended with His love.

4.10 One of the masters on love said, "Love is the hearts' delight in finding the beloved." Some say that love is the lover's belonging to his beloved in every way, and some say that love is the test of every noble lover based on his intentions; he whose intentions are the most exalted, his love is the purest. Some say that love is to be love-mad in the absence of the beloved, such that were one to catch sight of the beloved, one would be like a stammering drunkard. Some say that love is intoxication without sobering up, and utter astonishment when meeting the beloved, one that prevents any conscious perception. Some say that love is an affliction without hope of a remedy, and an illness with no known cure. It is said that love is a creditor who sticks to you and will not go away, and a spy from the beloved who knows every detail of your truthfulness throughout every state.

Al-Qushayrī mentions love in his *Subtleties of Mystical Allusions,* saying, 4.11

> The worshipper's love of God is a subtle state that he finds within himself. That state moves him to accept His command for him gladly, without aversion, for that state demands from him preference for Him, may He be praised, over everything and everyone else. Love stipulates that there never be in it any thought of one's own lot, for whoever has not ceased thinking of his own good fortune will not have even a sliver of love. God's love for His worshipper is His desire to be charitable and kind to him; it is His desire to bestow a special grace.[177]

Al-Rūdhbārī said, "If you do not leave all of yourself behind, you will never reach even the edge of love." Rābiʿah said, "The lover of God will never quiet his longing and sighing until he rests with his Beloved."[178] Abū ʿAbd Allāh al-Qurashī said, "True love is giving all of yourself to the one you love such that nothing remains of you that belongs to you."[179] Abū l-Ḥusayn al-Warrāq said, "Joy in God is from intense love of Him, and love is a fire in the heart consuming all impurities." Abū Yaʿqūb al-Sūsī said, "Love will never be right for you until you give up regard for love in exchange for regard for the Beloved, when all thought of love ceases."[180] Al-Junayd was asked about love, and he replied, "It is substituting the Beloved's attributes in place of the lover's attributes"—this is in accordance with the divine saying "And when I love him, I become his hearing and sight."[181] Al-Shiblī was asked about love, and he replied, "It is a cup holding a fire; when it settles in the senses and occupies the souls, they are annihilated." Al-Wāsiṭī said, "It is required of the lover that love's intoxications overwhelm him; if that does not happen, then it is not true love.[182]" 4.12

The master Abū l-Ḥasan al-Shādhilī, may God bless his inner heart, said, 4.13.1

> Love is a seizure sent by God to the heart of His believing worshipper, pulling him away from everything except Him. So you see his selfish nature inclining to obey Him, the intellect strengthened with mystical knowledge of Him, the spirit rapt in His presence, and the inner heart submerged in contemplation of Him. The worshipper asks for more, and it is granted as he enters into sweet, delicious love-talk with Him. Then he is clothed in the vestments of proximity on the carpet of nearness, and he comes to know the virginal realities and mature wisdoms. This is why the saints are called the brides of God, and none may look at the brides except their closest kin![183]

4.13.2 Someone asked him, "Now that I know about love, tell me, what are the drink of love and the cup of love? Who is the cupbearer? What are the taste, the drinking, the quenching, the intoxication, and the sobering up?" Al-Shādhilī replied,

> The drink is the light shining from the Beloved's beauty, whereas the cup is grace bringing that light to the mouths of the hearts. The Cupbearer is He who cares for his special elect and righteous worshippers; He is God, who knows the destinies and best interests of His beloveds. The one to whom that beauty is revealed, such that he enjoys something of it for a second or two before the veil is drawn over it, he is the craving taster. Whoever can maintain that for an hour or two, he is the true drinker. As for one to whom the matter occurs continuously, and the drinking lasts until his joints and veins are full of God's precious lights, that is the quenching. It sometimes happens that one loses all sense and reason, such that he does not understand what is being said or what he is saying; that is intoxication. Sometimes, as they perform recollection and pious acts of obedience, the cups are passed round to them, and their mystical states differ. They are not veiled from the divine attributes despite the overloading of their faculties. That is their time of sobriety, expansive vision, and increased

> knowledge. Thus, by the stars of knowledge and the moons of divine oneness, they are guided in their night, and they are illuminated during their day by the suns of mystical experience and knowledge: «They are the party of God! Will not the party of God be successful?»[184]

The master, ʿAbd al-Salām ibn Mashīsh, master of the master Abū l-Ḥasan al-Shādhilī, may God be satisfied with them both, said, 4.14.1

> Remain unsullied by polytheism; whenever you are polluted, purify yourself. Worldliness is a kind of filth. Whenever you tend toward lust, repair with repentance what you have ruined—or were about to ruin—with passion. Love of God is incumbent upon you out of respect and reverence. Become addicted to drinking cups of love with intoxication and sobriety. Whenever you awake and recover, drink until you are drunk and sober in Him, and until you are lost in His beauty without any thought of love or of drink, or of drinking or of the cup, by virtue of what appears to you of the light of His beauty and the perfect holiness of His splendor![185] Perhaps I am speaking to those who know nothing of love, or of the drink and the cup, or of intoxication and sobriety.

Someone said, "You are certainly right! Many are those who are deep into something without realizing that they are drowning. Enlighten and instruct me about what I do not know, or about what He has graciously granted me, even though I am heedless of it." Ibn Mashīsh replied, 4.14.2

> Perfect love is God's seizing the heart of one He loves by revealing to him the light of His beauty and the perfect holiness of His splendor. The drink of love is a mixing of attributes with attributes, traits with traits, lights with lights, names with names, qualities with qualities, and actions with actions. With this, the vision is expanded in those for whom God so wills. Drinking is giving the hearts, limbs, and veins a drink of this drink, such that

one becomes intoxicated, and the drinking becomes routine following training and practice. Each person is given a drink according to his measure. Among them are those who receive a drink without intermediary, since God, may He be praised, takes care of that for them. Others receive a drink from intermediaries, including angels, prophets, or the great learned scholars brought near to God. Still others are intoxicated by beholding the cup, without yet tasting anything. What then, do you think it will be like after one tastes the draught, drinks it down, and is quenched and intoxicated? After that, sobriety sets in to varying degrees, as is the case with intoxication.[186]

4.14.3 The cup is the True Reality's ladle, with which He serves that pure, unmixed, and clear drink to whomever He wills of His chosen worshippers among His creation. Sometimes, the drinker sees that cup as a physical form; another time, he may contemplate it abstractly, or he may perceive it intellectually. Physical forms are allotted to the instincts and bodies; the abstract form is allotted to hearts and minds, and intellectual form is allotted to spirits and the inner hearts. What a drink! How sweet! Blessed is one who drinks it continually and without interruption! We ask God for His grace: «That is the grace of God, which He gives to whomever He wills; He is ever present, all knowing!»[187] Sometimes, a group of lovers may gather and be given a drink from one cup; at other times, they are given a drink from many cups. One person may drink from one cup or many cups. Sometimes, drinks and cups will vary, just as drinking from one cup may vary, even though a multitude of lovers drink from it.[188]

4.15 Ibn ʿAṭāʾ Allāh al-Iskandarī has cited these straightforward statements by the two glorious spiritual authorities, may God sanctify their inner hearts, in his book *Subtleties of Divine Gifts* (*Laṭāʾif al-minan*). So reflect, may God show you mercy, on the mystical truths and divine mystical knowledge that they contain. You will find a discussion there of such clear explanation and discerning truth that the seeker will have no room for questioning. Success comes from God alone!

A concise definition of true love is found in the statement of the gnostic Abū l-ʿAbbās ibn al-ʿArīf, may God be satisfied with him, who writes, 4.16

> The love in the common folk is a love that sprouts from the appearance of divine grace, takes root by following Prophetic practice, and that grows in response to divine providence. It is a love that cuts off the Tempter, that makes service sweet, and that gives solace for misfortunes. On the path of the common folk, love is the support of faith. As for the love in the spiritual elite, it is a ravenous love that stifles expression, that suppresses allusion, and that is impossible to describe, for it is known only through bewilderment and silence. As has been said,
>
> She said (and I was already consumed
> by rapture and confusion
> when the two of us joined together
> after separation),
> "Aren't you the one,
> we are told,
> who loves to recall us,
> so why doesn't he ever remember us?"
> But rapture replied to her,
> "I have erased his memory,
> so nothing remains
> but sighs and confusion!"[189]

Ibn al-ʿArīf also wrote, "The true love of the spiritual elite is their annihilation in the True Reality's love for them, for all love is lost in the True Reality's love for His loved ones, «For after the True Reality, there is only being lost!»"[190]

4.17 Know, may God show you mercy, that what I have presented from the Qur'an, the prophetic traditions, and the words of the spiritual elite should suffice you. If you understand that, then know that one sign of love is just as one of them has said, "One who claims to love God without abstaining from what is forbidden him is an impostor! One who claims to love Paradise without giving charity is an impostor! One who claims to love His Emissary without loving poverty is an impostor!"[191] Bishr ibn al-Sarī said, "It is not a sign of love that you loathe what your beloved loves." Another said to one of his brothers, "Do you love God?" "Yes, by God!" he replied. The first man said, "Have you ever seen a lover who does not strive for his beloved's happiness?" Muḥammad ibn Yūsuf said, "The one who loves God loves the fact that people do not know him." Ibn ʿUyaynah said, "One who loves God loves those who love God." Fatḥ al-Mawṣilī said, "Preferring love of God over love of yourself is a sign of your love for God. The lover of God, in his love of God, never takes pleasure in this world below, nor does he neglect to remember God for even the blink of an eye!"

4.18 One sign of love is intimacy with Him and estrangement from all else. God revealed to Moses, prayers and peace be upon him, that a certain person was a perfect worshipper except for one fault: he enjoyed the breeze at dawn, which gave him peace. God said, "The one who loves Me finds peace in nothing else!" Another worshipper loved to listen to the song of a bird in a tree, so God revealed to their prophet as follows: "You loved to listen to a created thing, so I will certainly lower your rank; you will never regain it by anything that you do!"

4.19 When al-Junayd was asked about intimacy, he said, "It is the passing away of shame in the presence of reverence!" Abū l-Ḥusayn al-Warrāq said, "There is no intimacy with God without awe. When you are friendly with someone, you are no longer in awe of him. Yet with God the Exalted you will not increase in intimacy without increasing your reverence and awe of Him." Rābiʿah said, "Every lover is an intimate," and she recited,

I spoke to you within my heart,
while I left my body to one who sat near me.
So my body stayed with my companion,
while my heart's love was intimate there with me.

Mālik ibn Dīnār said, "The one who listens not to his dialogue with God but rather to his dialogue with created beings, knows little, his heart is blind, and his life ruined." Al-Kharrāz said, "Intimacy is the spirits' dialogue with the Beloved in gatherings of mystical proximity."[192]

Harim ibn Ḥayyān said, "I came to Uways who asked, 'What brings you here?' 'I came for your company,' I replied. Uways said, 'I have never understood how one can know God, yet seek the company of other than Him.'" A Sufi asked a woman who was one of the lovers, "Who is with you in the house?" So she replied, "Glory be to God, God is with me! I confide in Him, so how can I feel lonely, O servant of God, when He is my intimate friend?"[193] A Sufi was asked, "What keeps you from meeting with your brothers?" He replied, "My heart finds comfort with Him who knows my desire." 4.20

One sign of love is what Ibn 'Aṭā' said to one who asked him, "When does the worshipper reach the first stages of love?" He replied, "When he has five qualities, which are outwardly bitter but inwardly sweet: honoring covenants, keeping to the divine statutes, satisfaction with what is and patience with what is not, acceptance of what one has been assigned, and annihilation of selfishness in a struggle leading to extinction without end." 4.21

Another sign of love is acceptance. One gnostic said, "The lowest stage of love is that, were one's Beloved to throw him into Hellfire, his commitment to love would never waver." As has been said, 4.22

I stood begging at my Lover's door,
and He began to answer before I spoke:
"You are not who you think you are,
so die in rapture's being till you cease to be!

As best you can, keep up love for Me,
and I'll make My love wondrous in the world to come,
Where I will raise the veil of glory from Me,
for I love to honor the gnostics' plea.
Your cure lies with Me, but first, I'd love to see
you bedridden by love of Me!"

Dhū l-Nūn al-Miṣrī heard one of his ailing companions groan, and he said, "One is not truly in love if he does not relish heartache!" As has been said,

Don't be misled; the lover has signs
and messages of the beloved's gifts for him.
His bitter affliction is his comfort,
and his joy is in whatever his beloved does.
Denial from him is an acceptable gift,
while poverty is a tribute and ready favor.
From these signs, you will see him smile,
though his beloved leaves him with heartache.

4.23 One sign of love is preference for God over all else. Fatḥ al-Mawṣilī said, "Preferring love of God over love of yourself is a sign of your love for God." It was related that Moses son of ʿImrān, God's blessings be upon him, said, "O Lord, command me!" God answered, "I command you thrice regarding Me, that whatever happens to you, you should always prefer love of Me over all else. One who does not do so will have no mercy or prosperity from Me!"

4.24 Another sign of love is to persist in obedience. A Sufi said,[194]

You disobey God yet claim you love Him.
I swear that's a strange thing to say.
If your love were true, Him you would obey,
for the lover submits to the one he loves!

4.25 One sign of love is an inner heart free of this world and of the world to come. God revealed to Jesus, peace be upon him, "I examine the inner heart of My worshipper, and if I do not find in it love of this world or the Hereafter, then I fill it with My love and give him My protection."

4.26 Another sign of love is intense longing. Abū ʿUthmān al-Ḥīrī said, "Longing is the fruit of love. Whosoever loves God longs to meet Him. God the Exalted said, «The time appointed by God is near»[195] as solace for those who long. He is saying, 'I know the intensity of your longing for Me, so I have set an appointed time; when it arrives, you will meet the One for whom you long.'"[196] Dhū l-Nūn al-Miṣrī said, "Longing is the highest rank and highest mystical stage. When a person reaches it, he waits impatiently for death, longing for his Lord."[197] As ʿUmar al-Suhrawardī said, "Every lover is always longing, because the command of the True Reality, may He be praised, has no end. So whenever a worshipper reaches an end, he knows that beyond that is something greater and more perfect." Then he recited,

> My desire, like my love of you, has no end.
> One may reach it, but it has no end![198]

4.27 With regard to the statement in the Qur'ān «"I have run to you, my Lord, that You will be pleased"»[199] in an account by Moses, prayers be upon him, al-Wāsiṭī said, "That was out of longing for God and contempt for those behind him. «Moses said, 'They are right behind me,'»[200] for he was longing for conversation with God. So Moses threw down the tablets when he was out of time."[201] Fāris al-Dīnawārī said, "The hearts of those who long are illuminated by God's light. When they are stirred by longing, their light shines from east to west. God then presents them to the angels, saying, 'These are those who long for Me. I command you to bear witness that I long for them more.'" Al-Naṣrābādhī said, "All creatures have stages of longing, but not the stage of yearning. Whoever enters the stage of yearning is driven mad, leaving no trace or place behind." When Ibn ʿAṭāʾ was asked about longing, he replied, "A burning within, and hearts aflame and broken from separation after nearness!"

A Sufi was asked, "Which is greater, longing or love?" He replied, "Love, because longing is born of it, and no one yearns save one whom love has conquered. So love is the root, and longing is the branch."[202]

4.28 Ibn al-ʿArīf said,

> Longing is a stage for the common folk. As for the spiritual elite, in their opinion, it is a distressing defect inasmuch as longing is toward one who is absent. The orientation of this latter group is toward contemplation alone.[203] For them, the path is that the worshipper be absent while the True Reality is present, which leads to an understanding of the statement «And He is with you wherever you are!»[204] Longing, however, speaks of separation and alludes to one who is absent. A Sufi said,
>
> The longing complaint never makes sense
> to one always there to see.[205]

4.29 Similarly, when someone asked al-Anṭākī about longing, he replied, "A person only yearns for someone who is absent. I have never been without Him since I found Him." Al-Suhrawardī said, "I see no reason to reject longing completely. By longing, we only mean the quest that arises within for the original and highest share of nearness; this quest exists in lovers. Therefore, longing exists, and there is no reason to reject it."[206]

4.30 One sign of love is an inner heart free of everything but Him. God the Exalted revealed to David, peace be upon him: "O David, I forbade hearts to love Me along with anything besides Me!" In some traditions, God revealed to one of His prophets: "I single out for My love only the person who is not distracted from remembering Me, for he has only Me, and nothing of My creation is preferable to Me. Were he to be burned with fire, he would not feel the burning fire, and were he to be cut by saws, he would not find the touch of steel painful."

4.31 Another sign of love is love for those whom the Beloved loves. After her death, a prodigal woman was seen in a dream and was asked, "What did God do to you?" "He forgave me!" she replied. "For what reason?" she was asked, and she replied, "For my love of the Emissary of God, God bless and cherish him, and my desire to see him. I heard it proclaimed, 'Whosoever loves Our beloved and desires to see him, We spare from Our debasement and Our rebuke. Instead, We join him with the one he loves!'" How beautiful are these words:

For a single soul, a thousand nobles
stand guard and are sacrificed,
And so a thousand are honored
for the revered beloved![207]

One sign of love is the annihilation of everything in the beloved. Al-Rūdhbārī said, "As long as you do not purge your entire being, you will never reach even the edge of love." This is the stage of extinction in which consciousness is impossible, for though the body is present, sensation is gone. As has been said, 4.32

I erased my name and my body's trace,
so I disappeared from me while you stayed.
In my passing, my passing passed,
and in my passing, you were found!

In sum, the signs of love are innumerable, and what I have recounted is sufficient. 4.33

One tradition lauding the eminence of lovers is that Jesus, peace be upon him, passed by three persons whose bodies were emaciated and whose circumstances had changed for the worse, and he said, "Why do I see you in such a state?" When they replied, "Fear of Hellfire!" he said, "God has promised that one who fears will be safe." Then he left them and met three others whose emaciation was greater and whose circumstances were even worse, and he asked, "What has befallen you that I see you in such a state?" One of them replied, "Longing for His Garden and hope for His mercy!" and Jesus said, "God has promised that one who hopes shall receive." 4.34

Then he left them and met three others whose emaciation was far greater and whose circumstances were worse still, and he asked, "What has caused you to be in such a state?" They replied, "We love God and His Emissary!" and he said, "You are those brought near!"[208]

4.35 God revealed to one of His prophets as follows, "I have worshippers who love Me and whom I love; they long for Me, and I long for them; they remember Me, and I remember them. If you follow their way, I will love you, but if you turn away from them, I will loathe you!" He asked, "O my Lord, what is their distinguishing mark?" and God replied, "They track the shadows cast by the sun like the kindly shepherd watches his sheep, and they long for Me at sunset just as the birds long for their nests. When night falls, and it grows dark, and when every lover is alone with his beloved, they turn to Me and approach Me; they whisper to Me lovingly using My words, and they beseech Me for My grace, as they shout and cry, sigh, and suffer, and as they stand, sit, bow, and prostrate in prayer. I see what they endure on My account, and I hear when they ask for My love. The first thing I bestow on them is My light, which I throw into their hearts, so that they know Me as I know them. Second, if the seven heavens, the earth, and all they contain were weighed against them in the scale, I would deem it less than them. Third, when I turn My face toward them, you will see that each one I face will know what I want him to be given."[209]

4.36 One of Maʿrūf al-Karkhī's brothers asked him, "O Abū Maḥfūẓ, what spurred you to devotional practices and withdrawing from people?" He was quiet awhile and then replied, "Recollection of death." His questioner asked, "What constitutes recollection of death?" and he replied, "Recollection of the grave and judgment." "What constitutes recollection of the grave and judgment?" "Fear of Hellfire and hope for the Garden," he replied. His questioner said, "Why all this? If you love Him, He will make you forget all of this completely. When there is mystical knowledge between you and Him, He will suffice you in all things!"

A Sufi said, 4.37

> There is no benefit in a tree with no fruit, or in an oyster with no pearl, in bees with no honey, in a musk bag with no musk, in a husk with no seeds, in a body with no mind, in a mind with no heart, in a heart with no love, and in love with no nearness to the beloved. The value of the husks is in the seeds within them, and the value of men is in the hearts within them. The value of servants is in their masters, and the glory of the lovers is in their beloveds.

Sumnūn said, "The lovers have carried off all the honor of this 4.38
world and the next because the Prophet, God bless and cherish him, has said, 'Each man is with the one he loves, and these are with God the Exalted!'"[210] One gnostic described the mystical state of the lovers and their honor in attaining certain enlightenment, as follows:

> Love is renewed for them at every instant as they are in constant union. He shelters them with His protection by virtue of their serene dwelling in Him, such that their hearts moan and their spirits yearn with desire. Love and longing among them are signs sent by the True Reality regarding the truth of oneness, which is existence through God. Their desires thus disappear, and what appears to them from Him causes their hopes to cease. Were the True Reality to command all of the prophets to pray on behalf of these lovers, what the prophets would request for these lovers would be but a portion of what He has prepared for them with His foreknowledge in His primordial oneness and His everlasting eternity. For the lovers' share is their gnosis of Him, as their aims end in Him, and their desires unite in Him. Thus, of all the believers, the larger public envies them the most since He has taken away all of their cares. On this subject, someone recited,

My heart's desires were scattered, but drew together
  when my eyes saw You, my love.

I left others to their worldly life and faith,
devoting my love to You who are my world and creed.
So one I envied envied me as I became master of mankind
since You have mastered me!

4.39 An amazing story about love and lovers has been related by Sumnūn, may God be pleased with him, who said,

> I used to hear about a virtuous woman who lived in the desert. I sought her out several times, but could not find her. Later when I was on the Hajj pilgrimage alone, I met a disheveled, drunken, and confused woman, and I said to her, "What has happened to you?" "Ardent love!" she replied. "For whom?" I asked. "For One who has no direction to which I can point, nor any quality about which I can report," she replied. So I said, "Where will this lead?" and she replied, "To astonishment and bewilderment! Time after time I sought out the Kaaba until I heard within my inner heart that the Kaaba's knowledge of Him is like the whale's knowledge of Him under the seas, that the stars' knowledge of Him is like the earth's knowledge of Him. Then I reflected on the secret of my ardent love for Him around His Throne, and it called out to me saying, 'I seek that which you seek, and I am bewildered by what bewilders you!'" Sumnūn said, "Hearing her words intoxicated me! When I came to, I could not find her."

4.40 Dhū l-Nūn al-Miṣrī, may God be pleased with him, said,

> On the coast, I saw a young woman whose body bore the marks of ascetical struggles and whose face shone with the lights of contemplation. I said to her, "Where do you come from?" and she replied, "From the battleground of love!" "Where are you going?" I asked, and she replied, "To Him whose love has enslaved me, and whose essence is too holy for 'where' and far above 'how'! He is described only according to the worshipper's grasp and with the language of bewilderment and ineffability."

It has been related that Jesus, blessings and peace be upon him, passed by a monk's cell, where he found a pious worshipper whose back was bent and whose body was emaciated, for he had pushed ascetic practices to their limit. Jesus, blessings and peace be upon him, greeted him and said, "How long have you been in this cell?" and he replied, "For seventy years, I have asked God for one thing, which He has not granted me. Perhaps, O Spirit of God, you could intercede to see it granted." Jesus, peace be upon him, said, "What is that thing?" and the hermit replied, "That He grant me a taste of a tiny bit of His love." So Jesus, peace be upon him, prayed for that on his behalf. God then revealed to Jesus, "I have answered your prayer and accepted your intercession." Sometime later, Jesus, peace be upon him, returned to that place but did not find the man there. Instead, he saw that the cell had collapsed into a great rift. Jesus, peace be upon him, descended into the rift and continued for some miles. Then he saw the worshipper in a cave under the mountain, standing with his gaze fixed on the sky, mouth agape. Jesus, blessings and peace be upon him, greeted him but received no answer. Jesus, peace be upon him, was amazed by the hermit's condition, then God the Exalted, revealed, "O Jesus, he asked Us for an atom's weight of Our love, but We knew he was too weak for that. So We granted him a seventieth part of an atom, and with that, he is awestruck. What would his condition have been had We granted him more?"[211] 4.41

It has been related that Yaḥyā ibn Muʿādh al-Rāzī wrote as follows to Abū Yazīd al-Bisṭāmī, may God be pleased with them both: "I am drunk from all that I have drunk!" and Abū Yazīd wrote back, "Someone else has drunk the oceans of the heavens and the earth, but he is still not quenched, and his tongue hangs out as he asks, 'Is there more?'" He then recited the following on this subject: 4.42

I am amazed by one who says:
"I remembered my Lord."
Shall I forget so I can remember who I forgot?

I drank cup after cup of love,
and though the drink has no end,
I'm still not quenched![212]

4.43 What a difference there is between a worshipper who is too weak to bear even a seventieth portion of an atom of love, and a worshipper who drank the oceans of heaven and earth, but was still not quenched, and so he asked, "Is there more?" This is proof of the eminence of this community based on the Qur'an and the prophetic tradition. Eminence follows from that which is followed, and there is no doubt that the most perfect Muḥammadian essence is absolutely more eminent than the essences of a prophet, messenger, king, or archangel. Thus, his community is the most eminent of communities; those who are worthy of grace have the power to bear this love, while others chosen for love from outstanding communities that came before them were too weak to bear the least bit of love. This is because support for the Muḥammadian community came from his aid, and we mean by "his," the Chosen Prophet. So their strength comes from his strength, and success comes from God alone!

4.44 It has been related that a young man used to attend the teaching sessions of Dhū l-Nūn al-Miṣrī, may God be pleased with him. The young man was absent for a time before attending again, though now he had a sallow complexion and lean body. Dhū l-Nūn said, "O warrior, what gifts did the love of your Master bring you?" and he replied, "O teacher, do you think that a slave empowered by his master—who gave him the keys to his treasuries and confided the secret to him—do you think that slave would think it right to spread the secret?" He then recited the following:

They told him the secret,
and he tried but could not keep it.
So they'll never trust him with secrets
as long as he lives.

They stayed away from him,
so he did not enjoy their company
as their affection for him
turned to scorn.
People don't choose a gossip
to keep their secrets,
still less their love,
God forbid!

After his death, Bishr ibn al-Ḥārith was seen in a dream and was asked, "What became of Maʿrūf al-Karkhī?" Bishr shook his head and said, "How should I know? Barriers came between us, for Maʿrūf did not worship God out of fear of Hellfire, nor out of desire for His Garden; he only worshipped Him out of love and desire for Him. So, God raised him up to a most exalted company." Al-Junayd said, "Hellfire said, 'O Lord, if I do not obey You, will You punish me with something more severe than me?' He replied, 'Yes, I would have My greatest fire rule over you.' Hellfire asked, 'What is Your greatest fire? Is there a fire more awesome and severe than me?' and God replied, 'The fire of My love, which I have placed in the hearts of My intimate friends!'" ʿAbd al-Wāḥid ibn Zayd said, "I passed by a man sleeping in the snow, so I asked him, 'Aren't you cold?' and he replied, 'A person preoccupied with God's love does not feel the cold's sting.'" 4.45

A Sufi was asked, "How did you find love?" and he replied, "I stood on the shore of a vast sea, without a beginning or an end. The boat of 'one who draws near Me by the span of a hand, I will draw near him by the span of an arm'[213] drew near. So I sailed toward Him, as was right and proper, and the Spirit answered one who called it «In the name of God is its course and mooring.»[214] Then, when I was in the ocean's abyss, the sea lanes of love became rough, and this persisted until He gathered me into the collective sea of «He loves them, so they love Him.»[215] I am therefore between abiding and annihilation until I arrive at that annihilation." 4.46

4.47 How beautiful is what Ibn al-ʿArīf said on this:[216]

Say to one who claims our love
and pretends he's rooted to passion,
For if what he said were true,
then leaves would be on the bough:
"Where is wasting and fading away?
Where is burning love and restlessness?
Where is humility and flowing tears?
Where is anxiety and sleeplessness?"
Lovers plunge into passion's seas for us
when our fire flickers at nightfall,
And they turn their eyes toward it
and stand transfixed.
They pass the night as their states allow,
reaching the fire in different groups.
Though far from its light, some folk
follow the brightest paths,
While others approach close,
and are all enslaved to it,
And still other folk perish in the fire's light,
all consumed in the flames.
This is the final annihilation
telling of true abiding in True Reality!

4.48.1 ʿUthmān ibn Maysarah said,

> One day, I went into an asylum, and came upon a young man there with a dignified and noble quality about him, but he was staring at the floor without saying a word. As I watched him, he lifted up his head and began to smile. Then he looked to the sky, pointed up with both hands, and said,
>
> O sight of the eye and spirit of the heart,
> love of You threw me down to this place!

Yet command what You please, for acceptance demands
that glory and shame be bound together![217]

Then he wept and sighed over and over anxiously saying, "Alas! Alas!" Then he shouted out passionately:

I gave up my soul content with love of You,
content to be the ground for You to tread on.
I am content with what pleases You in love,
for I see love of You as a duty, and obedience to You
a command.
I close my eyes to all save You, and I look to no one
but You for the pleasure and pain I've seen.

Then he was overwhelmed as a mystical state came over him, and he spoke excitedly with the Lord of Glory, and I heard him say, "O my Master, delighted is the man who sees You, but disappointed is one who is distracted from You by something else. What is the Garden if not the contemplation of Your beauty, and what is Hellfire if not the inability to see Your perfection? How strange are hearts that do not see You or understand Your love talk. I swear by Your glory, O You most high, and by Your splendor, O Eternal One, were You to admit me into the Garden, only the vision of You would make it pleasant, and were You to throw me into Hellfire, I would not feel the pain, content with Your judgment. O my Master, how can the blessing of Your Garden distract me from You? It is only a diversion for those possessing a most refined nature, or a reward for those who did good deeds. How can the torment of Hellfire keep You away from me? It is only a lash upon those whose souls are bound to the prisons of their hopes. I did not worship You desiring the Garden, which is home to those who worked for it, nor out of fear of Hellfire, which is home to those who find agony there. How could one find the torture painful, when he contemplates Him who tortures, or how could one be distracted by beneficence, 4.48.2

when he sees the Benefactor in the blessings without a veil? O my Master, doing good deeds for a reward is the path of the wayfarers, but doing good deeds for You alone is the link for those who have arrived at union. How awesome is Your glory, how exalted Your greatness! I will never be content with this world or the next without You! By Your splendor, I have no escape from You whether I am in pain or pleasure!"

Then he screamed and grew agitated and, suddenly, he was dead.

4.49.1 Dhū l-Nūn, may God be pleased with him, is reported to have said the following:

I overheard the mystical recollection of a young woman who had arrived at union. I found her with an emaciated body in a ruined cloister; she wept often and was in a bewildered state. I stood there considering her situation, when I heard something of her conversations with God, as follows: "My Lord, by the truth of Your intimate friends, have mercy on me! For if You do not have mercy on me, then who will, O Beloved of the hearts?" Then she let out an intense sigh and fainted. When she recovered, I drew near and said, "Peace upon you, young woman," and she replied, "And upon you peace, Dhū l-Nūn." "How do you know my name?" I asked, and she replied, "Haven't you heard the statement:

Hearts are gathered in groups true to themselves
as the spirit of God decides.
Those who know each other are in harmony,
while those who don't, go their separate ways.

Dhū l-Nūn, our spirits roamed together in the World of Power, so we were made known to one another by the Living One who will never die."

4.49.2 Then I said, "Can't you find a place in which to live in this world other than a Christian cloister?" and she answered, "Dhū l-Nūn, mind your manners and think! Do you find anyone other than God in the universe?" "You are right," I replied, "But aren't you lonely?" and she said, "Dhū l-Nūn, is there an intimate friend other than God? How can a heart filled with the love of God fear any but God? This heart filled with the lights of God the Exalted, is like a lamp, with love as the chain holding it aloft, desire its wick, and oneness its light. Providence is its water on which floats its oil, which is mystical wisdom, whereas faith is the encompassing glass, and rapture its clarity. This is a heart that is close to God and intimate with God, whose love is for God, and whose ultimate return is to God. If selfish imaginings burn within it and extinguish its holy lights, then the breeze of providence moves upon it from the place of care and protection. Providence sways the chain, draws out the wick, and reignites the fire, causing the light to reappear, while replenishing the water, purifying the oil, and polishing the glass, thereby filling the heart with light upon light.[218] «He to whom God does not give His light, has no light.»"[219] Then she added, "Dhū l-Nūn, by Him who filled my heart with love of Him, who bestowed His pure providence upon me, and who dressed me in the vestments of His munificence, I give no mind to anything save God the Exalted!"

Then I said to her, "I see that you are eloquent with mystical wisdom, guide me to realization," and she replied, "Dhū l-Nūn, make constant vigilance your provision, make piety your mount, and make love your capital, until you reach a door with neither guard nor gatekeeper. When you arrive there, you will gain access to abiding, and you will win glorious good fortune and everlasting felicity!" Then she left me and never spoke to me again. I still regret her departure, may God be pleased with her.[220] 4.49.3

Al-Shiblī related the following story: 4.50

One year, I went on the Hajj pilgrimage and observed a woman who neither ate nor drank, because the love of

God had possessed her. She had no provisions and no riding animal. When she reached the place for consecration and ritual purity to begin the Hajj,[221] she said,

> What is in my heart melts my body,
>   and my heart melts from what the body holds.
> Cut my bond or, if you wish, grant union,
>   for whatever you do is fine with me.

When she reached the Kaaba, she called out:

> I am not one of the lovers
>   if I do not give up my heart and stay here!

Later, on the Plain of ʿArafāt, she became distressed because she had begun to menstruate. So she looked up into the sky and said, "You called me. But now that I have come, You forbid me?"

Al-Shiblī continued,

I was heartbroken for her, so I said, "Don't be sad. I have made the Hajj thirty times. I will gift them to you." Then she looked at me and said, "Shiblī, you are one of God's insignificant creatures, yet you offer me thirty Hajj pilgrimages. My Master is generous! Do you think, in view of His generosity, that He will not grant me a single Hajj? I will be patient for I have raised the issue with Him and await an answer." She had just sat down when a piece of green silk floated down. "Read it," she said, and it said, "In the name of God, the Compassionate and the Merciful. We have accepted you and forgiven you, and We have given you everything for your sake out of love for you!"

4.51 In sum, the stories of the lovers are many, but what I have related suffices. Success comes from God alone!

Epilogue on Love

At the conclusion of this book, God the Exalted inspired us with mystical truths, in both poetry and prose, regarding this very special love. They are appropriately placed here as an epilogue to this work. We ask God's help, and He «suffices us and is the best trustee»![222] 5.1

Know, may God show you mercy, that love is God's most wondrous secret. It is the result of being chosen, the effect of designation, the means to proximity, and the ascension to union. Love is pure grace, pure generosity, and true munificence. It is the secret of the inner heart and the subtlety of the divine command. It is an ocean without a shore, a jewel without a price, and a light without darkness. Love is a secret whose essence cannot be fathomed and a subtle meaning whose description cannot be grasped. «That is the grace of God, which He gives to whom He wills, and God possesses wondrous grace!»[223] 5.2

The quality of love is a fire that does not go out, a blaze that never dies. It is never-ending tears, an untreatable illness, an incurable disease. It is constant wasting away and incessant grief, a desire without solace, a never-ending passion, a persistent longing. As a result, restlessness builds up, breathing grows faster, confusion multiplies, and burning love increases. 5.3

The end result of love is total absorption, effacing the lover as his shadowy existence passes away with promised grace. Divine 5.4

providence sends him forth to those worthy of saintly sovereignty, with the realities of the attractions of oneness and the subtleties of eternity's breaths. No trace or word remains of anything else, indicating that the shadow of existence has disappeared in the rising sun of the witness to oneness. Then the tongue of glory recites in the presence of perfection, «Such is God, your true Lord, and after the True Reality, there is only being lost!»[224]

5.5 The following was composed by the very tongue of this mystical state:[225]

The worshipper vanished in true love,
gone from himself and all the worlds.
So there wasn't a jot of difference
to mark one off from another.[226]
Then with an epiphany, He revived one
He had effaced in Him, as difference disappeared,
And so with this promised gift,
He pleased the eyes and heart.

5.6 When God the Exalted wants to befriend one of His worshippers, He sends him the royal decree: «He loves them, so they love Him,»[227] together with the robe of honor: «God is pleased with them, and they are pleased with Him.»[228] Then the herald of protection will announce the bestowal of benefits: «Truly, they are the friends of God; they have no fear, nor will they grieve»[229]; and the sergeant-at-arms will sound off their honored designation: «They are the party of God! Will not the party of God be the successful ones?»[230] We have referred to this in verse, as follows:

They are the folk, God's people.
He bestowed loyalty upon them
as a robe of honor among His servants.
In His creation, He granted them His mercy
that they might help those they choose
with His overflowing love.

Love leads the lover to sacrifice all gain and confirms the gift of divine favor. Love is a seizure in many hearts, carrying away the lover's existence into the beloved. Love is not satisfied with the lover without his total sacrifice. Love's reality is a secret that attracts the inner heart and rules it; it captivates reason and seizes existence. It effaces being and annihilates everything. To define it is impossible, and allusion misses the mark; words fail and thought is frail; reason errs, and understanding is perplexed. It has been said that anyone who tries again and again to describe love will only end in failure. 5.7

The epiphany's sun rises in the inner hearts of the lovers, while the moon of nearness ascends in their spirits. Their hearts are flowing streams of grace; their minds are oceans filled with spiritual potential; their inner vision mirrors hidden revelation; their breasts contain volumes of inspired learning; their tongues are pens recording the eternal decree, and their ears ring with the pre-eternal message. Their concern is His love; their abode is with Him; their movement is His action; their silence is His command; their condition is to be near Him; their vision is His revelation, and their sight is His presence. Their support is His wine; their vision is His cups; their presence with the divine is their tavern, and their piety is His mark of friendship. Their existence is His gift; their manifestation is His mercy; their inner meanings are His attributes, and their reality is His essence. Their beginning is from Him, and their ending is with Him. They are madly in love with Him and dependent on Him. Their recollection of Him is their speech about Him. Their annihilation is in Him, and their abiding is with Him as He honors them. 5.8

God's saying «O My people»[231] is their protection; His saying «You will have no fear»[232] makes their joy permanent, and His saying «and you will not grieve»[233] undoubtedly alludes to some of what He holds in store for them. For He has said, «No one knows what joy lies hidden for them for what they have done.»[234] This makes clear that He has hidden away fine things: «A cup is passed round to them, filled from a flowing stream, pure, delicious to its drinkers, causing neither grogginess nor intoxication.»[235] The cup 5.9

is described as clear, and the drink is known for realization, while the place for drinking is the circle of divine selection, where the Cupbearer abides, of one essence, with everlasting attributes, abiding forever, most holy, of singular beauty, sovereign power, and eternal perfection. With His heady wine, He revives His lifeless companions, and with His countenance, He enlivens the lovers of His face.[236] All else is lacking in the presence of seeing Him, for the True Reality is present, and God is God!

5.10 One intoxicated by the drink of love can never recover. Its delight never turns to sorrow, for drinking it is felicity, and its exhilaration lasts for eternity. Its bliss is permanent, its joy abiding. Its clarity is widely described, and its bouquet is widely recognized; its mixed form is friendship; its pure form is true vision. We have alluded to this in verse, as follows:

An exalted drink beyond description
  of an eloquent report
    or symbolic speech.
He sends it round in the presence of realization
  in two cups:
    the power of glory and beauty's benevolence,
To the masters who disappeared
  in the folk's Cupbearer
    to live again with Him in a life without end.
So they are always with Him there
  in the garden of proximity
    where they have what they desire of union's bliss.

5.11 When God, the Glorious and Exalted, desires to unite a worshipper to true love, He takes hold of the reigns of firm resolve and leads him with the grace of kindness until He brings him to the ocean of love. Then, with the hand of divine selection, He casts him into the depths of providence within that sea, immersing him twice. The powerful immersion annihilates his existence, whereas the beautiful immersion preserves him in His love. The worshipper thereby realizes his existence and attains his farthest goal. We have alluded to this in verse:

> I see love,
> an ocean without a shore;
> if you are love's worthy one, dive in!
> Stay there
> until you drown in its depths,
> for there is no existence without love.
> There a brave one who disappears
> attains eternal life and wins the prize
> that he was once denied.
> He lives the heart's life
> in the garden of delight,
> a life of bliss for one who won God.
> All of his cares fall away
> in perpetual joy and happiness
> here to stay.
> How lovely is eternal life!
> The worshipper who wins it
> is fortunate, indeed.
> For the servant is in bliss
> forever near Him,
> safe from separation's fire.
> This station is attained
> only by the chosen lover;
> only one He has blessed will win it.
> For He has saved him from himself and existence
> and revealed to him rare loveliness
> as he came to know.
> With His command, He entrusts him
> to act on His behalf in all the world,
> giving him the secret hidden from others.

So seek out him
who has come to His sea.
If you are love's worthy one, dive in!

5.12 The lover's heart is the place of vision. If God makes it worthy to receive the gift of realization, He removes from it the filth of otherness, sweeping away from it the desolation of difference. Then He fills the heart with the light of love and reveals to it the true essence. He is his ear and his eye, so by Him, he hears and sees; he hears His address, and he beholds His beauty.[237] So he has no sign of the world or news of himself, as nothing remains of otherness, nor any trace of difference. We have alluded to this in verse:

His epiphany appeared to him,
so he became an eye to see and behold
the subtle sense of His loveliness.
Yet grace appears only to one pure without,
while the secret is found
only with one true within.

5.13 Love is an adornment that does not appear on one whose ambition hangs on others. For how could one lay claim to it while he gives himself completely to others? He will never taste the flavor of passion while clinging to someone other than God. Rather, as much as you can forget yourself, you will recollect God, and to the extent of your love, you will love. Observe how sound is the divine saying to which I referred earlier:[238]

> One who draws near to Me by a hand span, I will draw near to him by an arm's length, and he who draws near to Me by an arm's length, I will draw near to him by the span of open arms. If he walks toward Me, I will run to him.

We give good advice with our allusions in the following verses:

Beware of loving anyone save Him
who owns your entire affair.

For you are from Him, returning to Him;
so, my brother, be with Him and for Him.
Strive hard to make devotion to Him
the heart's affair.
Don't turn away to another
and so debase Him.
Don't tend toward others
and fill your heart with them.
Don't look to another with the heart's eye,
and so lead it astray.
Don't turn your ear from Him
to listen to the blamer—avoid him!
But if he comes blaming you,
come down hard on him and say:
"I'll never renounce Him
who blessed one like me with being.
All others are nothing, for my love
is the True Reality who raised my rank high!"

You, love's pretender, where are your wasting away and your anguish? Where are your burning passion and your dismay? Where are your longing and your yearning? Where are your craving and your groaning? Where are your grief and your sighing? Where are your agony and your ardent love? Where is your taking leave of yourself? Where is your fleeing from yourself? Where is your annihilation in your beloved? Where is your effacement in the one you seek? Don't you know that one who claims to love requires clear proof for his claim? Clear proofs include always being restless with anxiety, unceasing anguish, flowing tears, and loss of appetite. No remnant remains of you, not even a splinter of your existence. If you prove to have these outstanding traits without any sign or trace of love for another, then your claim to love is true, as we have expressed in the following verses: 5.14

One who claims to love his Master
    must bring proof to prove his claim true.
Among these proofs is longing without end,
    and desire and yearning when He is recalled.
Tear ducts are never dry around dewy eyes,
    while sleepless lids cruelly lash his slumber.
One grows thin, lips are parched, one burns within;
    the mind is unsteady, never forgetting thought of Him.
One is dazed and confused with anxiety,
    worn out by love's torment and grief.
He gives himself away, caring nothing
    for any share in this world or the next.
He abstains from everything save the Beloved,
    truly choosing what his Master prefers for him.
This is evidence that love's claim is true,
    and I mean the love of one content with his Master.
He reveals his love when he ends in love,
    as all that is left of him disappears,
Until, his effacement complete, the Beloved's face
    appears to him, and that visage renews his life.
He lives with God, a joyful life without end,
    absorbed in the light of His shining face,
Forever, in the gardens of proximity,
    quenched by union's cups with a pure heady wine,
Enjoying union forever, forever in bliss,
    gazing at Him in love-talk.
How wondrous are cups giving rise to pleasure
    bringing joy to His companions' intoxication.
They are drunk on cups of love
    in the tavern of realization as He pleases.
O masters, their portion is from Him,
    for their share is no one save Him!

Love is God's grace. The worshipper cannot attain it by means of great effort, nor by a clever stratagem that he took great pains to devise, nor by means of a good deed that he has perfected, nor by weighty knowledge that he has mastered, nor due to some power on which he relies, nor any exalted lineage that he may have. How could this be? Love is, after all, pure grace, pure generosity. God chooses whichever worshipper He pleases for it. This love forgives sins, covers faults, exalts the humble, raises the fallen, returns one from exile, and reunites one who was cut off. Such is God's love for his worshipper. As for the worshipper's love for God, it is a secret that seizes him completely and draws all of him, until it rejoins him to his Lord and seats him in His presence; it causes him to pass away from his ephemeral self, and this passing leads him to abide in His essence. 5.15

The subtle meaning of God's love for the worshipper is the selection of the worshipper for this secret—which we have noted and to which we have referred—by seizing him with the Beloved's attractions and effacing annihilations until the worshipper is without a sense of self in the light of the sun of true oneness. This is the true realization of true love. Anything less than this love is a love dependent on causes and contingencies derived from attention to the pursuit of pleasure and the avoidance of pain. 5.16

How lovely is the statement by the illustrious spiritual axis, the master, Muḥammad ibn Abī l-Wafāʾ, may God sanctify his heart: 5.17

I had reckoned that union with you
could be bought
with expensive goods and slaves.
Yet foolishly I thought
your love was not worth
the waste of precious souls.
But then I saw you choose
and bestow wondrous gifts
on the one you loved,

And then I knew you could not be had
by any clever deal,
so I hung my head in shame.

5.18 The close presence to God is the lovers' paradise; union's wine is their nectar, and the perpetual beatific vision is their bliss. They are delighted in the garden of the beatific vision, enjoying the fruits of the divine address.[239] They renounced this world and turned away from the world to come; they had no place of refuge save the exalted nearness of perfect proximity to God. «They are those whom God has guided, and they are those with insight.»[240] God established a relationship with them with «He loves them, and they love Him,»[241] at the place of «God is pleased with them, and they are pleased with Him,»[242] on the carpet of «Truly, they are the friends of God; they have no fear nor will they grieve.»[243] God greeted them with the greeting: «"Peace," a word from a merciful Lord,»[244] and He gave them «what souls desire and eyes find sweet.»[245] He chose them for nearness «in truth to a mighty King,»[246] and granted them bliss as «their Lord quenched them with a pure drink.»[247] He made them immortal in the garden of the beatific vision «where they will have what they desire, and We have still more!»[248] This, by God, is the honor attained by the highest aims and the gift received by the greatest aspirations. «That is the grace of God, which He gives to whom He will, and God possesses wondrous grace!»[249]

5.19 Regarding this topic, it is appropriate that we cite our verse inspired by God, as follows:

God looked with favor on a folk,
so they stayed away
from worldly fortunes.
In love and devotion, they worshipped Him;
they surrendered themselves
with the best intention.

They gave themselves up to Him in love
    and passed away from existence
        with nothing left behind.
Then with kindness and compassion,
    He turned to them
        and revealed to them His essence,
And they lived again
    gazing at that living face
        as His eternal life appeared.
They grazed near Him[250]
    in the garden of union,
        and drank from contemplation's cups
Filled as promised
    with a pure wine
        from the vision of true oneness.
Oh how they drank it,
    cups of pure wine
        bringing good cheer.
It gave them
    never-ending happiness
        in a tranquil life of pleasant union
Where fears and doubts fled away
    as protection arrived
        against the veil of difference.
So here's to good health,
    glad tidings, and blessings
        for reaching the wish and the goal:
A union without separation,
    and a vision
        never to be concealed!
After this, by God, there is no desire,
    no, nor aim
        for a pure spirit.

So they were pleased with their good fortune:
union with the Lover
who chose them above all others,
As He gave them His love
and fulfilled His promise
in the holy presence.
They were chosen by Him
as His vice-regents
and raised in rank to help others.
So under their banner stands
all existence where their command
is carried out at once.
They are His people
due to His grace upon them,
while all others are but strangers.
They appeared in existence
bearing largesse
to all the worthy ones.
So among humanity,
they are chosen suns,
whom only the blind deny.
They are the masters!
I was joined to them
and we stood alone in oneness,
And drank the wine, not from cups,
but from jars, in the tavern
where the oath was sworn.[251]
We drank it until we were drunk
in pre-eternity where drunkenness
lasts forever.
So you see us drunk on wine,
though appearing sober
to disguise the affair.

And gracing us by passing round wine
    is the most praised noble one,
        Muḥammad, chosen from the best,
The grace of God, His mercy for us,
    the noblest of creation,
        the best of humanity's best,
The best of servants,
    to whom He revealed the Book
        and gave the special gift of prophecy.
He is the light of our eyes,
    who grants our desires,
        the secret of secrets of those who give aid.
May the Beloved's blessings,
    ample peace, and cheer
        flow over him
And his progeny, companions, and family
    for they are a folk to whom
        we have a sublime connection,
As long as the cups
    come round to us
        and quench our thirsty hearts,
As long as our Beloved reveals Himself,
    and we behold in this epiphany
        true oneness!

The end of this poem marks the end of this book, all with the support of the Giver of Gifts, the Sovereign. Praise God as He deserves, and may His prayers and peace be upon the perfect and glorious master, the noblest in all the worlds, Muḥammad, and upon his family and companions. May He grant them salvation, honor, and glory! I entrust to God the Exalted my faith, my self, my children, my husband, those dear to me in God, and all that He has bestowed on me and them, in religion and in this world and the next. I ask 5.20

Him to pardon me, my parents, and all Muslim men and women, with His grace and generosity, for He is the most merciful! I turn my face toward God seeking the intercession of the most noble of His nobles, our most wondrous means to God, Muḥammad, the chosen one, may God bless and cherish him, that He might always grant me, my children, and the ones I hold dear in Him, the favor of seeking His aid and succor, and the beatific vision of Him in intimacy with Him in His presence, in total union with Him, without any affliction accompanying it whatsoever. He is always magnanimous and generous, kind and merciful![252]

Notes

1 Q Āl ʿImrān 3:173.

2 Q Nūr 24:31.

3 Q Hūd 11:90.

4 Q Taḥrīm 66:8.

5 Q Ḥujurāt 49:11.

6 Q Baqarah 2:222.

7 Cf. ʿAbd al-Qādir al-Jīlānī, *Ghunyah*, 1:129–30; Holland, *Sufficient Provision*, 2:105–7.

8 Cf. al-Qushayrī, *Risālah*, 1:276; Knysh, *Epistle*, 111.

9 Cf. al-Ghazālī, *Iḥyāʾ*, 4:32; Stern, 89.

10 Cf. al-Ghazālī, *Iḥyāʾ*, 4:44; Stern, 105.

11 Q Muṭaffifīn 83:14.

12 Cf. al-Qushayrī, *Risālah*, 1:284, who ascribes this saying to Dhū l-Nūn; Knysh, *Epistle*, 115.

13 Rābiʿah al-ʿAdawiyyah implies that while one may ask forgiveness for past sins with one's tongue, the tendency toward sin remains within one's selfish nature requiring further penance. Cf. al-Ghazālī, *Iḥyāʾ*, 4:47, 49; Stern, 109, 113.

14 Cf. al-Ghazālī, *Iḥyāʾ*, 4:12; Stern, 48.

15 Cf. al-Ghazālī, *Iḥyāʾ*, 4:14; Stern, 52.

16 Cf. al-Ghazālī, *Iḥyāʾ*, 4:14; Stern, 52.

17 Cf. al-Qushayrī, *Risālah*, 1:287; Knysh, *Epistle*, 117.

18 Cf. al-Kalābādhī, 93; Arberry, 83; al-Sarrāj, 68.

19 Cf. al-Sarrāj, 68; al-Qushayrī, *Risālah*, 1:283; Knysh, *Epistle*, 115.

20 Cf. al-Sarrāj, 69; al-Qushayrī, *Risālah*, 1:284–85; Knysh, *Epistle*, 115.

21 Cf. al-Kalābādhī, 93; Arberry, 83.

22 Cf. al-Qushayrī, *Risālah*, 1:281; Knysh, *Epistle*, 114.

23 Cf. al-Kalābādhī, 93; Arberry, 83. Also see al-Qushayrī, *Risālah*, 1:283; Knysh, *Epistle*, 115.

24 Cf. al-Ghazālī, *Iḥyāʾ*, 4:3–4; Stern, 32. Also see comments on repentance by the Sufi master Sahl al-Tustarī (d. 283/896) in his commentary on Q Tawbah 9:112; Keeler, 85–86.

25 Cf. al-Sarrāj, 68; al-Qushayrī, *Risālah*, 1:282–83; Knysh, *Epistle*, 114–15.

26 Q Nūr 24:31.

27 The paragraph is nearly a verbatim quotation from al-Qushayrī's commentary on Q Nūr 24:31; see al-Qushayrī, *Laṭāʾif*, 2:608.

28 Cf. al-Sulamī, *Ḥaqāʾiq*, 1:74.

29 See al-Qushayrī, *Risālah*, 1:286; Knysh, *Epistle*, 117. Also, cf. Q Tawbah 9:119: "So He turned to them that they might turn in repentance."

30 A similar statement is ascribed to Dhū l-Nūn by ʿAṭṭār; see Losensky, 180.

31 Q Baqarah 2:222.

32 Q Tawbah 9:117.

33 Tradition has it that this occurred when Muḥammad was a young shepherd boy; see Guillaume, 71–72.

34 Cf. al-Sulamī, *Ḥaqāʾiq*, 1:290.

35 Cf. al-Tustarī's statement in his commentary on Q Tawbah 9:112; Keeler, 85.

36 Probably the noted Sufi al-Ḥusayn ibn Manṣūr al-Ḥallāj.

37 Cf. al-Qushayrī, *Risālah*, 1:286; Knysh, *Epistle*, 116; ʿAbd al-Qādir al-Jīlānī, *Ghunyah*, 132–33; Holland, *Sufficient Provision*, 2:117; and al-Ghazālī, *Iḥyāʾ*, 4:5; Stern, 35.

38 Cf. a similar account in al-Ghazālī, *Iḥyāʾ*, 4:51; Stern, 118.

39 Cf. al-Qushayrī, *Risālah*, 2:469 for a similar statement ascribed to al-Tustarī.

40 Also quoted by al-Iṣfahānī, 9:379.

41 The implication here is that if the sinner does not repent before death, he will have no second chance when he stands before God on Judgment Day.

42 For this last statement cf. al-Qushayrī, *Risālah*, 1:345; Knysh, *Epistle*, 144.

43 Cf. a similar account in al-Iṣfahānī, 9:365–66.

44 The poet alludes to a tradition of the prophet Muḥammad, who is reported to have said, "I know God better than you do, and I fear Him more than you do!" See al-Qushayrī, *Laṭā'if*, 3:409.

45 The opening verses of this poem refer to the Hajj, whose stopping places include al-Khayf and Minā, as well as the Plain of ʿArafāt where pilgrims pray to God for forgiveness.

46 That is to say, the poet is not enamored of an earthly beloved, and so remembering the alighting places of the Hajj pilgrimage reminds him only of God.

47 Cf. al-Qushayrī, *Risālah*, 1:54; Knysh, *Epistle*, 18.

48 Cf. al-Qushayrī, *Risālah*, 1:85; Knysh, *Epistle*, 30.

49 Q Mujādilah 58:22.

50 Q Kahf 18:44.

51 Q Ḥajj 22:5.

52 Q Baqarah 2:222.

53 Q Qiyāmah 75:36.

54 Q Ṭūr 52:21.

55 Q Zumar 39:58.

56 Q Āl ʿImrān 3:178.

57 Q Yūsuf 12:64, 92.

58 Cf. ʿĀ'ishah al-Bāʿūniyyah, *Dīwān*, 128.

59 In the first and final verse of this poem, ʿĀ'ishah al-Bāʿūniyyah refers to the hadith "I am with My servant who thinks of Me," which she cited earlier in her discussion of repentance.

60 Q Zumar 39:2.

61 Q Zumar 39:11.

62 Q Bayyinah 98:5.

63 Cf. a different version of the same tradition in ʿAbd al-Qādir al-Jīlānī, *Ghunyah*, 2:78; Holland, *Sufficient Provision*, 3:344.

64 Cf. ʿAbd al-Qādir al-Jīlānī, *Ghunyah*, 2:76; Holland, *Sufficient Provision*, 3:341.

65 Q Kahf 18:110.

66 For a similar tradition cf. ʿAbd al-Qādir al-Jīlānī, *Ghunyah*, 2:77; Holland, *Sufficient Provision*, 3:343.

67 Cf. ʿAbd al-Qādir al-Jīlānī, *Ghunyah*, 2:78; Holland, *Sufficient Provision*, 3:346.

68 Cf. ʿAbd al-Qādir al-Jīlānī, *Ghunyah*, 2:76; Holland, *Sufficient Provision*, 3:340.

69 Q Muʾminūn 23:1.

70 Cf. ʿAbd al-Qādir al-Jīlānī, *Ghunyah*, 2:78; Holland, *Sufficient Provision*, 3:346.

71 This is probably Aḥmad ibn ʿĀṣim al-Anṭākī who is reported to have said, "The most beneficial sincerity is that which is free of hypocrisy, self-adornment, and affectation." See al-Sulamī, *Ṭabāqāt*, 138; Knysh, *Islamic Mysticism*, 38–39.

72 Probably ʿIkrimah al-Madanī.

73 Cf. ʿAbd al-Qāḍir al-Jīlānī, *Ghunyah*, 2:73; Holland, *Sufficient Provision*, 3:332.

74 Probably Makḥūl al-Shāmī.

75 Q Kahf 18:110.

76 Cf. al-Qushayrī, *Risālah*, 2:446; Knysh, *Epistle*, 221–22; ʿAbd al-Qādir al-Jīlānī, *Ghunyah*, 2:75; Holland, *Sufficient Provision*, 3:335; and al-Sulamī, *Ḥaqāʾiq*, 2:192.

77 Cf. al-Qushayrī, *Risālah*, 2:443; Knysh, *Epistle*, 220.

78 Cf. al-Qushayrī, *Laṭāʾif*, 3:232, which omits the negative particle *lā*, and gives the verb in the third person. Thus, this saying reads, *wa-yuqālu huwa an yulāḥiẓa maḥalla l-ikhtiṣāṣi*, i.e., "It is said, '[Sincerity] is that one beholds the place of distinction.'" This statement implies that one who has sincerity has been given a place among the spiritually elect, one possible meaning of the term *al-ikhtiṣāṣ*. However, another meaning of *al-ikhtiṣāṣ*, also used by al-Qushayrī (*Laṭāʾif*, 3:367), is to seek worldly distinction, and ʿĀʾishah al-Bāʿūniyyah later cites this quotation as well. In the manuscript of the *Selections*, the negative particle *lā* appears to have been added as an editorial correction.

79 Al-Qushayrī, *Laṭāʾif*, 3:232.

80 Cf. al-Qushayrī, *Laṭā'if*, 3:267.

81 Cf. al-Qushayrī, *Risālah*, 1:167, 2:445; Knysh, *Epistle*, 64, 221; ʿAbd al-Qādir al-Jīlānī, *Ghunyah*, 2:74; Holland, *Sufficient Provision*, 3:333; al-Sulamī, *Ḥaqā'iq*, 2:194.

82 Cf. ʿĀ'ishah al-Bāʿūniyyah, *Dīwān*, 129.

83 Cf. ʿAbd al-Qādir al-Jīlānī, *Ghunyah*, 2:74; Holland, *Sufficient Provision*, 3:331.

84 Cf. al-Qushayrī, *Risālah*, 2:444; Knysh, *Epistle*, 221; ʿAbd al-Qādir al-Jīlānī, *Ghunyah*, 2:73; Holland, *Sufficient Provision*, 3:331.

85 Cf. a similar statement ascribed to al-Junayd; al-Qushayrī, *Risālah*, 2:446; Knysh, *Epistle*, 221.

86 Cf. ʿAbd al-Qādir al-Jīlānī, *Ghunyah*, 2:74; Holland, *Sufficient Provision*, 3:33; al-Sulamī, *Ḥaqā'iq*, 1:194.

87 Cf. ʿAbd al-Qādir al-Jīlānī, *Ghunyah*, 2:73; Holland, *Sufficient Provision*, 3:332.

88 Cf. al-Qushayrī, *Risālah*, 2:445–46, 448–49; Knysh, *Epistle*, 221–23.

89 Q Āl ʿImrān 3:173.

90 ʿĀ'ishah al-Bāʿūniyyah, *Dīwān*, 129.

91 Q Tawbah 9:109.

92 Q Mā'idah 5:100.

93 Q Ghāfir 40:19.

94 Q Saba' 34:3.

95 Q Rūm 30:4.

96 Q Nisā' 4:108.

97 Al-Damīrī, 2:10, and abridged by ʿĀ'ishah al-Bāʿūniyyah.

98 ʿĀ'ishah al-Bāʿūniyyah, *Dīwān*, 129.

99 Q Baqarah 2:152.

100 Al-Qushayrī is probably referring to the Sufi doctrine known as "Day of the Covenant," based on Q Aʿrāf 7:172, when God first spoke to the spirits of all humanity in pre-eternity. There, God's remembrance of humans brought them into existence; see Schimmel, 171–72.

101 Cf. al-Qushayrī, *Laṭā'if*, 1:137–38.

102 Al-Qushayrī, *Laṭā'if*, 1:137, which reads, "Be consumed in Our existence, and We will remember you after your annihilation from yourselves."

103 Al-Sulamī, *Ḥaqā'iq*, 1:78.

104 Q Baqarah 2:152.

105 Q Baqarah 2:152.

106 Q Aḥzāb 33:41.

107 Al-Qushayrī, *Laṭā'if*, 3:164.

108 Q Raʿd 13:28.

109 Q Raʿd 13:28.

110 Al-Qushayrī, *Laṭā'if*, 2:229–30.

111 That is to say, even the advanced mystical state of a tranquil heart is a veil between the believer and the oneness of God. Here, ʿĀ'ishah al-Bāʿūniyyah paraphrases a statement on types of hearts that al-Sulamī ascribed to Muḥammad ibn Mūsā al-Wāsiṭī; al-Sulamī, *Ḥaqā'iq*, 1:334.

112 Q Isrā' 17:11.

113 Q Raʿd 13:28.

114 Probably al-Ḥusayn ibn Manṣūr al-Ḥallāj.

115 Cf. al-Sulamī, *Ḥaqā'iq*, 1:334.

116 Q ʿAnkabūt 29:45.

117 Several verses of the Qur'an, including Q Aḥzāb 33:41–42, command believers to remember God, thus rendering remembrance a religious obligation and an act of obedience.

118 Cf. al-Qushayrī, *Laṭā'if*, 3:99: "It is said that God's remembrance of you is greater than your remembrance of Him."

119 That is to say, the worshipper is mystically consumed in the remembrance of God.

120 Cf. al-Qushayrī, *Laṭā'if*, 3:99.

121 Q ʿAnkabūt 29:45.

122 Q Baqarah 2:152.

123 Q Kahf 18:24.

124 Al-Kalābādhī, 103–4; Arberry, 95.

125 Cf. al-Qushayrī, *Risālah*, 2:464–69; Knysh, *Epistle*, 233–35.

126 Al-Kalābādhī, 104; Arberry, 95.

127 Cf. al-Qushayrī, *Laṭā'if*, 1:137.

128 Cf. al-Qushayrī, *Risālah*, 2:524–25; Knysh, *Epistle*, 272–73.

129 Cf. al-Qushayrī, *Risālah*, 2:466; Knysh, *Epistle*, 233.

130 Cf. al-Qushayrī, *Risālah*, 2:468; Knysh, *Epistle*, 234.

131 Cf. al-Qushayrī, *Risālah*, 2:466; Knysh, *Epistle*, 233.

132 Q Muḥammad 47:19.

133 Q Muḥammad 47:19.

134 Cf. al-Qushayrī, *Laṭāʾif*, 1:196. Here, al-Qushayrī appears to allude to the "Tradition of Willing Devotions," often quoted by Sufis, in which God says, "My servant draws near to Me by nothing more dear to Me than the religious obligations that I have imposed on him, and My servant continues to draw near Me by willing acts of devotion such that I love him. Then when I love him, I become the ear with which he hears and the eye with which he sees." See Schimmel, 43.

135 Q Āl ʿImrān 3:1–2. This Qurʾanic passage opens with the Arabic letters *alif lām mīm*. A total of twenty-nine chapters of the Qurʾan begin with these or other letters, which are known as "the opening letters" or "the disconnected letters." Their meaning and intention remain a mystery; see *EQ* 3:471–77.

136 Cf. al-Qushayrī, *Laṭāʾif*, 1:218.

137 Q Āl ʿImrān 3:18.

138 Q Āl ʿImrān 3:18.

139 Cf. al-Qushayrī, *Laṭāʾif*, 1:226.

140 Q Muḥammad 47:19.

141 Cf. al-Qushayrī, *Laṭāʾif*, 3:410–411, and *Risālah*, 1:218; Knysh, *Epistle*, 85.

142 Q Anʿām 6:91.

143 Q Baqarah 2:152.

144 This verse is from a love poem by Abbasid poet and literary scholar Ibn al-Muʿtazz (d. 296/908); see Ibn Khallikān, 3:78. Al-Ghazālī later quoted this verse to convey the ineffable quality of the mystical experience; see his *al-Munqidh min al-ḍalāl*, 129; Watt, 64. As a result, some later authors have incorrectly ascribed the verse to al-Ghazālī. For the poem, see Jacobi, 35–56.

145 Q Ikhlāṣ 112:1.

146 Q Kahf 18:44.

147 Q Qāf 50:35.

148 Cf. ʿĀʾishah al-Bāʿūniyyah, *Dīwān*, 139. "Saʿd" is the name of a Sufi novice, real or fictitious, whom ʿĀʾishah al-Bāʿūniyyah advises in several poems.

149 Cf. ʿĀʾishah al-Bāʿūniyyah, *Dīwān*, 137.

150 Q Āl ʿImrān 3:31.

151 Cf. al-Qushayrī, *Laṭāʾif*, 1:235.

152 Cf. verses by Sarī al-Saqaṭī in al-Qushayrī, *Risālah*, 2:619; Knysh, *Epistle*, 331.

153 Q Ibrāhīm 14:36.

154 Q Āl ʿImrān 3:31.

155 In Islamic tradition, "the dear friend" (*al-khalīl*) is an epithet for the prophet Abraham, while "the beloved" (*al-ḥabīb*) is an epithet for the prophet Muḥammad. By contrast, "the Beloved" refers to God.

156 Q Āl ʿImrān 3:31.

157 Cf. al-Qushayrī, *Laṭāʾif*, 1:235–36.

158 Cf. al-Qushayrī, *Risālah*, 2:612–14; Knysh, *Epistle*, 327–28, for further discussion of the etymology of the term *maḥabbah* ("love").

159 Cf. al-Qushayrī, *Laṭāʾif*, 1:235–36.

160 Cf. al-Qushayrī, *Sharḥ*, 130–31.

161 Q Tīn 95:4.

162 Q Muʾminūn 23:12.

163 Q Māʾidah 5:54.

164 Q Māʾidah 5:54. Cf. al-Qushayrī, *Laṭāʾif*, 1:431–33.

165 Q Māʾidah 5:54.

166 Q Māʾidah 5:54.

167 Q Māʾidah 5:54.

168 Q Māʾidah 5:54.

169 Cf. al-Suhrawardī, 455.

170 Q Māʾidah 5:54.

171 Q Māʾidah 5:54.

172 Q Māʾidah 5:54.

173 Also quoted by al-Suhrawardī, 454.

174 Also quoted by al-Suhrawardī, 454.

175 Also quoted by al-Iṣfahānī, 1:108.

176 Cf. al-Qushayrī, *Risālah*, 2:610–11; Knysh, *Epistle*, 325–26. For this divine saying, also see Graham, 173–74.

177 Cf. al-Qushayrī, *Laṭā'if*, 1:235. Also see al-Qushayrī, *Risālah*, 2:611–12; Knysh, *Epistle*, 326–27.

178 Cf. al-Suhrawardī, 456–457.

179 Cf. al-Qushayrī, *Risālah*, 2:615; Knysh, *Epistle*, 328, and al-Suhrawardī, 457.

180 Cf. al-Suhrawardī, 457–458.

181 Cf. al-Suhrawardī, 457; al-Qushayrī, *Risālah*, 2:615; Knysh, *Epistle*, 328. This is a reference to the "Tradition of Willing Devotions" mentioned earlier.

182 Cf. al-Suhrawardī, 459, 455.

183 Cf. Ibn 'Aṭā' Allāh, 52; Roberts, 65; Douglas, 144–45.

184 Q Mujādilah 58:22, and also see An'ām 6:97: «And He it was who made for you the stars that you may be guided by them in the darkness on land or sea.» Cf. Ibn 'Aṭā' Allāh, 53; Roberts, 65–66; Douglas, 145.

185 Cf. Ibn 'Aṭā' Allāh, 53–54; Roberts, 66–68; Douglas, 143.

186 Cf. Ibn 'Aṭā' Allāh, 54; Roberts, 68–69; Douglas, 143–44.

187 Q Mā'idah 5:54.

188 Cf. Ibn 'Aṭā' Allāh, 54–55; Roberts, 69; Douglas, 144.

189 Cf. Ibn al-'Arīf, 68–69. Also cf. al-Anṣārī, 88–90.

190 Q Yūnus 10:32, and cf. Ibn al-'Arīf, 84–85.

191 Cf. al-Suhrawardī, 457.

192 The sayings in this section may be found in al-Suhrawardī, 462.

193 Cf. al-Suhrawardī, 462.

194 Cf. al-Suhrawardī, 458, who ascribes these verses to Rābi'ah al-'Adawiyyah.

195 Q 'Ankabūt 29:5.

196 Cf. al-Suhrawardī, 459–60; al-Qushayrī, *Risālah*, 2:630; Knysh, *Epistle*, 338.

197 Cf. al-Suhrawardī, 460.

198 Cf. al-Suhrawardī, 459.

199 Q Ṭā Hā 20:84.

200 Q Ṭā Hā 20:84, and cf. al-Qushayrī, *Risālah*, 2:628; Knysh, *Epistle*, 337.

201 Cf. al-Suhrawardī, 460.

202 Cf. al-Suhrawardī, 461; al-Qushayrī, *Risālah*, 2:627–30; Knysh, *Epistle*, 336–37.

203 Cf. al-Anṣārī, 91.

204 Q Ḥadīd 57:4.

205 Cf. Ibn al-ʿArīf, 76–79.

206 Cf. al-Suhrawardī, 461.

207 Cf. al-Suhrawardī, 455.

208 In the Qur'an, «those brought near» (*al-muqarrabūn*) refers to those believers given an exalted place in Paradise; e.g. Q Wāqiʿah 56:10–12.

209 Cf. al-Ghazālī, *Iḥyā'*, 4:315.

210 Cf. al-Suhrawardī, 458.

211 Cf. Ibn al-ʿArīf, 70–73.

212 Cf. al-Qushayrī, *Risālah*, 2:620; Knysh, *Epistle*, 331–32.

213 For this frequently quoted divine saying, see Graham, 175.

214 Q Hūd 11:41.

215 Q Mā'idah 5:54.

216 Cf. Ibn al-ʿArīf, 86–91. In this poem, Ibn al-ʿArīf probably alludes to the story of God's appearance as the Burning Bush found in the Qur'an: Q Ṭā Hā 20:9–36; Naml 27:7–10.

217 Cf. Q Āl ʿImrān 3:26: «You exalt whom You please, and You debase whom You please. Good is in Your hands, for You are, indeed, omnipotent!»

218 Cf. the famous "Light Verse," Q Nūr 24:35. Regarding the shape and design of lamps from the Mamlūk period, see Behrens-Abouseif, esp. 6–7.

219 Q Nūr 24:40.

220 Cf. a similar story in Tāqī al-Dīn al-Ḥiṣnī's *Siyar al-ṣāliḥāt* as noted in Smith, 233.

221 The *iḥrām* is a state of ritual purity required of all pilgrims to Mecca. Pilgrims usually enter this state at one of the designated stations on the roads leading into Mecca. This account also makes reference to several places on the Hajj including the Kaaba and Abraham's Station (*maqām Ibrāhīm*) near the Kaaba, and to "Standing" on the Plain of ʿArafāt; see von Grunebaum, 15–49.

222 Q Āl ʿImrān 3:173.

223 Q Ḥadīd 57:21 and Jumuʿah 62:4.

224 Q Yūnus 10:32.

225 That is, ʿĀʾishah al-Bāʿūniyyah claims to have composed these verses while in a mystical state or *ḥāl*.

226 Literally, "There was no mark to denote difference; so the letter *ʿayn* could not be distinguished from the letter *ghayn*." The difference between the two letters is a single dot.

227 Q Māʾidah 5:54.

228 Q Bayyinah 98:8; Māʾidah 5:119; Mujādilah 58:22.

229 Q Yūnus 10:62.

230 Q Mujādilah 58:22.

231 Q Zukhruf 43:68; also see ʿAnkabūt 29:56, and Zumar 39:55.

232 Q Zukhruf 43:68; also see Aʿrāf 7:49.

233 Q Zukhruf 43:68; also see Aʿrāf 7:49.

234 Q Sajdah 32:17.

235 Q Ṣāffāt 37:45–47.

236 Cf. Ibn al-Fāriḍ, *Naẓm al-sulūk*, verse 1.

237 Here, ʿĀʾishah al-Bāʿūniyyah again refers to the "Tradition of Willing Devotions" and to Q Aʿrāf 7:172, which contains God's first address to humanity in pre-eternity: «Am I not your Lord?»

238 That is, section 1.5 in *Principles of Sufism*.

239 Cf. Q Rūm 30:17; Aʿrāf 7:172.

240 Q Zumar 39:18.

241 Q Māʾidah 5:54.

242 Q Māʾidah 5:119; Mujādilah 58:22; Bayyinah 98:8.

243 Q Yūnus 10:62.

244 Q Yā Sīn 36:58.

245 Q Zukhruf 43:71.

246 Q Qamar 54:55.

247 Q Insān 76:21.

248 Q Qāf 50:35.

249 Q Ḥadīd 57:21.

250 Cf. the prophetic tradition, which ʿĀʾishah al-Bāʿūniyyah cited earlier in section 3.23 of *Principles*: "If you pass by the meadows of the Garden, graze there."

251 In vv. 23–24, ʿĀʾishah al-Bāʿūniyyah again refers to Q Aʿrāf 7:172 and the covenant God made with humanity in pre-eternity when He said, «Am I not Your Lord?» to which they responded, «Yes, indeed, we so witness.»

252 The following citation is found at the end of the manuscript: "This copy of this book was completed at the beginning of the month of Jumādā al-Ūlā, in the year one thousand and seventy one after the Prophet's emigration [AD 1661] by the hand of the unworthy ʿAbd al-Raḥīm ibn ʿAlī, known by his family name, Ibn Maksab, may God pardon him, his parents, and all Muslims. Amen."

Glossary of Names and Terms

ʿAbd Allāh ibn ʿAlī al-Tamīmī Abū Naṣr al-Sarrāj (d. 378/988) an influential Sufi and scholar, and author of the Sufi manual *Kitāb al-Lumaʿ* (see *EI2*, 9:65–66, and Knysh, *Islamic Mysticism*, 118–20).

ʿAbd Allāh ibn Busr (d. 88/707) an occasional companion of the prophet Muḥammad (see al-Dhahabī, 3:430–33).

ʿAbd Allāh ibn Masʿūd (d. 32/652) a companion of the prophet Muḥammad (see *EI2* 3:873–75).

ʿAbd al-Salām Ibn Mashīsh (d. 625/1234) an ascetic and Sufi of Fez and among the most important spiritual guides of Abū l-Ḥasan al-Shādhilī (see Knysh, *Islamic Mysticism*, 208).

ʿAbd al-Wahhāb al-Bāʿūnī (d. 925/1519) son of ʿĀʾishah al-Bāʿūniyyah (see Homerin, "Living Love," 215, and "Writing," 393, 396).

ʿAbd al-Wāḥid ibn Zayd al-Baṣrī (d. ca. 150/767) a preacher and early Muslim ascetic associated with a very early Sufi cloister on ʿAbbādān, an island in the Shaṭṭ al-ʿArab near Basra (see Knysh, *Islamic Mysticism*, 16–18).

Abraham (Ar. Ibrāhīm) in Islam, a prophet and father of the Arabs through his first son Ishmael (Ar. Ismāʿīl). Abraham is often referred to as al-Khalīl ("the friend") based on Q Nisāʾ 4:125: «And God took Abraham as a friend (*khalīl*)» (see Glassé, 18–19).

Abū ʿAbd Allāh al-Qurashī (fl. fourth/tenth century) an early Sufi of Basra (see Karamustafa, 121).

Abū ʿAbd al-Raḥmān al-Sulamī see Sulamī, Abū ʿAbd al-Raḥmān al-.

Abū l-ʿAbbās ibn al-ʿArīf (d. 536/1141) a Sufi and scholar of Andalusia, spending much of his time teaching students at Alería. He was the author of a mystical treatise entitled *The Beauties of Spiritual Sessions* (*Maḥāsin al-majālis*) (see Ibn al-ʿArīf, 8–19, and Renard, 50–51).

Abū l-Dardāʾ see Uwaymir ibn Zayd.

Abū l-Ḥasan al-Shādhilī (d. 656/1258) a Sufi from North Africa and progenitor of the Shādhiliyyah Sufi order, which spread throughout North Africa, Spain, Egypt, and Syria (see Knysh, *Islamic Mysticism*, 207–12).

Abū l-Ḥusayn al-Dīnawārī This is perhaps Abū l-Ḥasan ʿAlī al-Dīnawārī (d. 330/941), a Sufi master of Egypt (see Knysh, *Epistle*, 59).

Abū l-Ḥusayn al-Warrāq (d. ca. 320/932) an early Sufi of Nishapur (see al-Sulamī, *Ṭabāqāt*, 299–301).

Abū l-Mukhāriq cited by Ibn Abī l-Dunyā (d. 281/894) for a tradition of the prophet Muḥammad.

Abū l-Shaykh al-Iṣbahānī see Iṣbahānī, ʿAbd Allāh ibn Muḥammad al-.

Abū l-Qāsim al-Qushayrī (d. 465/1072) a Sufi and scholar who wrote extensively on Sufism. His works include his Sufi manual, the *Epistle* (*Risālah*), as well as a mystical commentary on the Qur'an entitled *The Subtleties of Mystical Allusion* (*Laṭāʾif al-ishārāt*), both important sources for succeeding generations of Sufis, including ʿĀʾishah al-Bāʿūniyyah (see Knysh, *Islamic Mysticism*, 130–32, and *Epistle*, xxi–xxvii).

Abū ʿAlī al-Daqqāq (d. ca. 405/860) a Sufi and al-Qushayrī's spiritual master and father-in-law (see Knysh, *Epistle*, xxi–xxii).

Abū Bakr al-Kattānī, Muḥammad ibn ʿAlī (fl. third/tenth century) a Sufi of Baghdad and a companion of al-Junayd (see al-Sulamī, *Ṭabaqāt*, 3:73–77).

Abū Bakr al-Ṣiddīq (d. 13/634) one of the prophet Muhammad's closest companions, his father-in-law, and the first caliph after the Prophet's death. Abū Bakr was famous for his asceticism and faith in God (see *EI2* 1:109–11).

Abū Bakr ibn al-ʿArabī (d. 543/1148) a scholar and judge who wrote a number of books on hadith, jurisprudence, the Qur'an, and history (see *EI2* 3:707).

Abū Bakr ibn Dāwūd (d. 806/1403) a Sufi shaykh of the ʿUrmawī branch of the Qādiriyyah order (see Homerin, "Living Love," 213).

Abū Dāwūd (d. 275/889) author of the *Book of Traditions* (*Kitāb al-Sunan*), a canonical collection of Sunni hadith (see *EI2* 1:114).

Abū Dharr (d. 32/652) an early convert to Islam and a companion of the prophet Muḥammad (see *EI2* 1:114–15).

Abū Hurayrah (d. ca. 58/678) a companion of the prophet Muḥammad and a prolific source for traditions from the Prophet (see *EI2* 1:129).

Abū Mūsā al-Ashʿarī (d. 42/662) a younger companion of the prophet Muḥammad, who later served as the governor of Basra and Kufa (see *EI2* 1:695–96).

Abū Naṣr al-Sarrāj see ʿAbd Allāh ibn ʿAlī al-Tamīmī.

Abū Saʿīd al-Kharrāz (d. 277/890) a noted early Sufi and author of the *Book of Truthfulness* (*Kitāb al-Ṣidq*) (see Knysh, *Islamic Mysticism*, 57–60).

Abū Saʿīd al-Khudrī (d. 74/693) a companion of the prophet Muḥammad and a legal scholar in the nascent Muslim community (see al-Dhahabī, 3:168–72).

Abū Umāmah see Asʿad ibn Sahl al-Anṣārī.

Abū ʿUthmān al-Ḥīrī, Saʿīd ibn Ismāʿīl (d. 298/910) an ascetic and early Sufi master among the Malāmatiyyah who spread Sufism in Nishapur (see al-Sulamī, *Ṭabaqāt*, 170–75, and Karamustafa, 48–51).

Abū Yaʿlā, Aḥmad ibn ʿAlī (d. 307/919) a scholar of hadith and author of hadith collection entitled *Large Work of Traditions* (*al-Musnad al-kabīr*) (see Kaḥḥālah, 2:17–18).

Abū Yaʿqūb al-Makfūf cited by ʿAbd al-Qāḍir al-Jīlānī (d. 561/1166) for a saying on sincerity.

Abū Yaʿqūb al-Sūsī (fl. fourth/tenth century) a Sufi contemporary of al-Junayd (see Knysh, *Epistle*, 64).

Abū Yazīd al-Bisṭāmī (d. ca. 261/875) an early Sufi famous for his esoteric sayings on union and oneness (see *EI2* 1:162–63).

Adam the "father of humanity" who was taught the names of all things by God (see *EI2* 1:178–79).

Aḥmad al-Bazzār (d. 292/905) a scholar of hadith and author of a collection entitled *The Traditions* (*al-Musnad*) (see al-Dhahabī, 13:554–57).

Aḥmad ibn ʿĀṣim al-Anṭākī (d. 220/835) a Sufi and scholar who wrote on proper conduct and mystical life (see al-Sulamī, *Ṭabaqāt*, 138, and Knysh, *Islamic Mysticism*, 38–39).

Aḥmad ibn Ḥanbal (d. 241/855) the eponym of the Ḥanbalī school of law and author of *The Traditions* (*al-Musnad*), a canonical collection of Sunni hadith (see *EI2* 1:272–77).

Aḥmad ibn Muḥammad al-Nūrī (d. 295/907) a Sufi who stressed love of God and His mercy for humanity (see Schimmel, 60–61).

Aḥmad ibn Muḥammad Ibn Naqīb al-Ashrāf (d. 909/1503) the husband of ʿĀʾishah al-Bāʿūniyyah (see Homerin, "Living Love," 214–15, and *Emanations*, 14–15).

ʿAlī ibn Abī Ṭālib (d. 40/660) the cousin and son-in-law of the prophet Muḥammad, the fourth Sunni caliph and the first Shiʾa imam (see *EI2* 1:381–86).

Anas ibn Mālik (d. 91–93/709–11) a companion of the prophet Muḥammad and a source for many traditions regarding the Prophet (see *EI2* 1:482).

Anṭākī al- see Aḥmad ibn ʿĀṣim al-Anṭākī.

Anṣārī, ʿAbd Allāh al- (d. 481/1089) a noted Hanbalī jurist and Qādirī Sufi, who wrote several mystical works (see *EI2* 1:515–16).

Asʿad ibn Sahl al-Anṣārī, Abū Umāmah (d. 100/718) born during the Prophet's lifetime, he related hadith from many of the prophet Muḥammad's companions (see al-Dhahabī, 3:517–19).

Ayyūb al-Sakhtiyānī (d. ca. 131/748) a religious scholar who related hadith (see al-Iṣfahānī, 3:3–15, and al-Sulamī, *Ṭabaqāt*, 452).

Barakah (b. 899/1491) a daughter of of ʿĀʾishah al-Bāʿūniyyah (see Homerin, "Living Love," 215).

Bayhaqī, Aḥmad ibn al-Ḥusayn al- (d. 458/1066) a prolific scholar of hadith and the author of *The Large Traditions* (*al-Sunan al-kubrā*) (see *EI2* 1:1130).

Bazzār al- see Aḥmad al-Bazzār.

Bishr ibn al-Ḥārith (d. 227/842) known as "the barefoot" (al-Ḥāfī), Bishr was among the early ascetics of Basra and Baghdad (see Knysh, *Islamic Mysticism*, 48–52).

Bishr ibn al-Sarī (d. 195/813) a Sufi and preacher who spent time in Basra (see al-Sulamī, *Ṭabaqāt*, 98).

Bukhārī, Muḥammad al- (d. 256/870) author of the canonical hadith collection *The Sound Traditions* (*al-Ṣaḥīḥ*), and one of the most respected authorities of Sunni hadith (see *EI2* 1:1296–97).

Būṣīrī, Muḥammad al- (d. 694/1295) author of the poem *The Mantle Ode* (*al-Burdah*), the most celebrated panegyric to the prophet Muḥammad [see *EI3* (2010) 1:171–72].

Ḍaḥḥāk ibn Qays al-Fihrī (d. 64/684) a companion of the prophet Muḥammad, who related a few traditions from him (see *EI2* 2:89–90, and al-Dhahabī, 3:241–45).

Damīrī, Muḥammad al- (d. 808/1405) a scholar and Sufi, most famous for his encyclopedia of animals entitled *The Lives of Animals* (*Ḥayāt al-ḥayawān*) (see *EI2* 2:107–8).

David (Ar. Dāwūd) in Islam, a prophet and king who brought the Psalms as a revelation from God (see Glassé, 94–95).

Dāwūd al-Ṭā'ī (d. 165/781) a Muslim ascetic (see Knysh, *Islamic Mysticism*, 13, 24).

Dhū l-Nūn al-Miṣrī (d. 246/861) an ascetic and mystic regarded as one of the first Sufis to systematize the mystical states and stages on the path to gnosis (see *EI2* 2:242).

Dīnawārī al- see Abū l-Ḥusayn al-Dīnawārī or Fāris al-Dīnawarī.

Fāris al-Dīnawarī (d. ca. 340/951) a Sufi mentioned by al-Qushayrī (see al-Qushayrī, *Risālah*, 629–30; Knysh, *Epistle*, 338).

Fatḥ al-Mawṣilī (d. 220/835) an early Sufi of Baghdad and a companion of al-Sarī al-Saqaṭī (see Knysh, *Epistle*, 382).

Fuḍayl ibn 'Iyāḍ (d. 187/803) an ascetic and Sufi who also studied hadith (see *EI2* 2:936).

Gabriel (Ar. Jibrīl/Jibrā'īl) in Islam, the Spirit of Revelation who brought the Qur'an from God to Muḥammad, regarded as an archangel (see Glassé, 136).

Ghawrī, Qānṣūḥ al- (d. 922/1516) one of the last Mamlūk sultans, he reigned 906–22/1501–16 (see Petry, 119–232).

Ḥākim al-Naysābūrī, Muḥammad ibn ʿAbd Allāh al- (d. 405/1014) a judge and hadith scholar whose writings include *Knowledge on the Science of Hadith* (*Maʿrifat ʿulūm al-ḥadīth*) (see *EI2* 3:82).

Ḥallāj al- see al-Ḥusayn ibn Manṣūr al-Ḥallāj.

Harim ibn Ḥayyān (d. ca. 26/646) an early figure of Muslim piety and a companion of Uways al-Qaranī (see al-Dhahabī, 4:48–50, al-Kalābādhī, 24, and Arberry, 8).

Ḥasan al-Baṣrī al- (d. 110/728) a noted ascetic, preacher, and theologian (see *EI2* 3:247–48).

Ḥudhayfah al-Marʿashī (d. 192/808 or 207/823) a Sufi and companion of the noted legal scholar Sufyān al-Thawrī (d. 162/778) (see al-Iṣfahānī, 8:267–71, and al-Munāwī, 1:188–89).

Ḥudhayfah ibn al-Yamān (d. 37/657) an ascetic who related a number of hadith regarding the prophet Muḥammad (al-Dhahabī, 2:361–69).

Ḥusayn al-Maghāzilī al- (fl. fourth/tenth century) a Sufi and acquaintance of Ruwaym ibn Aḥmad (d. 303/915) (see al-Kalābādhī, 146–47, and Arberry, 149).

Ḥusayn ibn Manṣūr al-Ḥallāj al- (d. 309/922) a controversial Sufi who was executed by political authorities in Baghdad (see *EI2* 3:99–104).

Ibn Abī l-Dunyā (d. 281/894) a prolific scholar and teacher noted for his piety (see *EI2* 3:684).

Ibn Ajā see Maḥmūd ibn Muḥammad ibn Ajā.

Ibn al-ʿAbbās, ʿAbd Allāh (d. ca. 68/687) a cousin of the prophet Muḥammad and often considered the father of Qurʾanic exegesis (see *EI2* 1:40–41).

Ibn al-ʿArīf see Abū l-ʿAbbās ibn al-ʿArīf.

Ibn al-Fāriḍ, ʿUmar (d. 632/1235) the greatest Arab Sufi poet and author of the Sufi classic *Poem of the Sufi Way* (*Naẓm al-sulūk*) (see Homerin, *ʿUmar Ibn al-Fāriḍ*).

Ibn ʿAṭāʾ Allāh al-Iskandarī (d. 709/1309) an important Egyptian Sufi and preacher, and author of a number of works, including *Subtleties of Divine Gifts* (*Laṭāʾif al-minan*), which relates the words and teachings of Sufi masters of the Shādhiliyyah Sufi order (see Knysh, *Islamic Mysticism*, 208–13).

Ibn Ḥanbal see Aḥmad ibn Ḥanbal.

Ibn Ḥibbān, Muḥammad (d. 354/965) a prolific author, well respected for his collection of hadith entitled *The Sound Traditions* (*al-Musnad al-ṣaḥīḥ*) (see *EI2* 3:798).

Ibn Jarīr al-Ṭabarī see Muḥammad ibn Jarīr al-Ṭabarī.

Ibn Mājah, Muḥammad (d. 273/887) a scholar of hadith who composed the *Book of Traditions* (*Kitāb al-Sunan*), a canonical collection of Sunni hadith (see *EI2* 3:856).

Ibn Mas'ūd see 'Abd Allāh ibn Mas'ūd.

Ibn Manṣūr see al-Ḥusayn ibn Manṣūr al-Ḥallāj.

Ibn Mashīsh see 'Abd al-Salām Ibn Mashīsh.

Ibn 'Umar, 'Abd Allāh (d. 73/693) son of the second caliph, noted for his piety and knowledge of traditions of the prophet Muḥammad (see *EI2* 1:53–54).

Ibn 'Uyaynah, Sufyān (d. 196/812) a jurist and scholar of the traditions of the prophet Muḥammad (see Kaḥḥālah, 4:235).

Ibrāhīm al-Khawwāṣ (d. 291/904) a Sufi and friend of al-Junayd and al-Nūrī (see Knysh, *Epistle*, 56).

Ibrāhīm al-Tayyimī (fl. second/eighth century) an ascetic who also transmitted hadith (see al-Munāwī, 1:149–50).

Ibrāhīm ibn Adham (d. ca. 162/778) a celebrated ascetic (see Knysh, *Islamic Mysticism*, 21–22).

'Ikrimah al-Madanī (d. 105/723) an early Qur'anic exegete (see al-Iṣfahānī, 3:326–47, and Kaḥḥālah, 6:290).

'Irbāḍ ibn Sāriyah al- (d. 75/694) a companion of the prophet Muḥammad and a member of the People of the Bench (*Ahl al-Ṣuffah*), a group of pious poor in Medina (see al-Dhahabī, 3:419–22, and Schimmel, 28).

Iṣbahānī, 'Abd Allāh ibn Muḥammad Abū l-Shaykh al- (d. 369/979) composed a number of works on Qur'anic commentary, history, and hadith, including his *History of the Traditions* (*Kitāb al-Tā'rīkh 'alā l-sunan*) (see Kaḥḥālah, 6:114).

Iskandarī al- see Ibn 'Aṭā' Allāh al-Iskandarī.

Israfel (Ar. Isrāfīl) in Islamic tradition, an archangel who reads out the divine decrees in heaven and who will blow the trumpet signaling the start of the Day of Judgment (see *EI2* 4:211).

Jābir ibn ʿAbd Allāh (d. 78/697) a companion of the prophet Muḥammad and a legal scholar (see al-Dhahabī, 3:189–94).

Jamāl al-Dīn Ismāʿīl al-Ḥawwārī (d. 900/1495) mystical guide to ʿĀʾishah al-Bāʿūniyyah and her husband, and a member of the Qādiriyyah Sufi order (see Homerin, "Living Love," 213–14, and *Emanations*, 13–14).

Jesus (Ar. ʿĪsā) son of Mary, in Islam, a prophet celebrated for his asceticism and miracles (see Glassé, 208–9).

Junayd al-Baghdādī al- (d. 297/910) one of the most influential spiritual masters of the Sufi tradition. He was the nephew and disciple of Sarī al-Saqaṭī (see *EI2* 2:600, and Knysh, *Islamic Mysticsm*, 52–56).

Jurjānī, ʿAlī al- (d. 816/1413) a scholar who wrote on logic, theology, and Sufism (see *EI2* 2:602–3).

Kalābādhī, Abū Bakr al- (d. 380/990) a scholar of Sufism and author of *Introduction to the Doctrines of the Sufis* (*al-Taʿarruf li-madhhab ahl al-taṣawwuf*) (see Arberry, ix–xv; Knysh, *Islamic Mysticism*, 123–24).

Kharrāz al- see Abū Saʿīd al-Kharrāz.

Luqmān mentioned in the Qur'an as a man given great wisdom by God, which he passed on to his son (Q Luqmān 31:12–19) (see *EI2* 5:811–13).

Maḥmūd ibn Muḥammad ibn Ajā (d. 925/1519) confidential secretary and foreign minister to the Mamlūk sultan al-Ghawrī (see Homerin, "Living Love," 215–16).

Makḥūl al-Shāmī (d. 116/734) a jurist and hadith scholar noted for his piety (see al-Iṣfahānī, 5:177–93, and al-Dhahabī, 5:155–60).

Mālik ibn Dīnār (d. ca. 131/748) an ascetic and preacher (see *EI2* 6:266–67).

Mamlūks the ruling dynasty of Egypt and greater Syria founded by royal slave soldiers (*mamlūk*) who succeeded their Ayyūbid masters in 648/1250. The Mamlūk dynasty came to an end with their defeat by the Ottomans in 923/1517.

Maʿrūf al-Karkhī (d. 200/815) a preacher and ascetic who lived in Baghdad, and stressed the importance of good deeds for a pious life. He is considered one of the early founders of Sufism (see Knysh, *Islamic Mysticism*, 48–49).

Michael (Ar. Mīkāl/Mīkhā'īl) an archangel mentioned in Q Baqarah 2:92. In Islamic tradition, he is often an associate of Gabriel (see *EI* 5:491–92).

Moses (Ar. Mūsā) in Islam, a prophet and lawgiver sent by God to the Jews; he freed them from Pharaoh and their Egyptian captivity. Later, Moses spoke with God at Sinai and on the occasion of the Burning Bush. Moses is often referred to as *Kalīm Allāh* ("the one to whom God spoke") based on Q A'rāf 7:143: «His Lord spoke to him (*kallamahu*)» (see Glassé, 275).

Mu'ādh ibn Jabal (d. 17/638 or 18/639) a companion of the prophet Muḥammad noted for his asceticism (see Ibn al-'Imād, 1:29–30).

Mu'āwiyah ibn Abī Sufyān (d. 60/680) a scribe to the prophet Muhammad and, later, caliph and founder of the Umayyad dynasty (see *EI2* 7:263–69).

Muḥammad (d. 10/632) son of 'Abd Allāh and a member of the Quraysh tribe in Mecca. He is the prophet of Islam to whom God sent the Qur'anic revelations through Gabriel until Muḥammad's death in Medina (see Guillaume).

Muḥammad ibn Abī l-Wafā' (d. 891/1486) a Sufi author and poet contemporary with 'Ā'ishah al-Bā'ūniyyah. He was a member of the Wafā'ī Sufi order and spent time in Jerusalem and Cairo (see al-Sakhāwī, 7:196).

Muḥammad ibn Jarīr al-Ṭabarī (d. 310/923) a celebrated historian and Qur'an exegete, who also compiled a collection of hadith (see *EI2* 10:11–15).

Muḥammad ibn Mūsā al-Wāsiṭī (d. 320/932) a Sufi and student of al-Junayd (see Knysh, *Epistle*, 58).

Muḥammad ibn Yūsuf this is perhaps Muḥammad ibn Yūsuf al-Bannā' (d. ca. 365/976), a Sufi mentioned by al-Qushayrī (see al-Qushayrī, *Risālah*, 2:678; Knysh, 370).

Muḥyī al-Dīn Yaḥyā al-'Urmawī see Yaḥyā al-'Urmawī.

Muṣ'ab ibn 'Umayr (d. 3/625) a close companion of the prophet Muḥammad who was martyred at the Battle of Uḥud while defending the Prophet. Muṣʿab went from a refined life in pagan Mecca to one of poverty after converting to Islam. He was noted for his piety, and was sent by the Prophet to Medina to spread the news of Islam and to read the Qur'an among the pagan tribes in order to seek their conversion (see al-Dhahabī, 1:145–48, and al-Iṣfahānī, 1:106–8).

Muslim ibn al-Ḥajjāj (d. 261/875) a scholar of hadith who compiled traditions in his *The Sound Collection of Traditions* (*al-Jāmiʿ al-ṣaḥīḥ*), a canonical collection of Sunni hadith (see, *EI2* 7:691–92).

Nahrajūrī, Isḥāq ibn Muḥammad al- (d. 330/941) a Sufi and student of al-Junayd (see Knysh, *Epistle*, 64–65).

Nasāʾī, Aḥmad al- (d. 303/915) author of *The Traditions of al-Nasāʾī* (*Sunan al-Nasāʾī*), a canonical collection of Sunni hadith (see *EI2* 7:969–70).

Naṣrābādhī, Ibrāhīm ibn Muḥammad al- (d. 367/977) a scholar of hadith, a Sufi of Khurasan, and a student of al-Shiblī (see Knysh, *Epistle*, 10–11, 72–73).

Nawawī, Yaḥyā al- (d. 676/1277) a prolific author and a noted scholar of hadith and Shāfiʿī jurisprudence (see *EI2* 7:1041).

Naysābūrī al- see Ḥākim al-Naysābūrī, Muḥammad ibn ʿAbd Allāh al-.

Nūrī al- see Aḥmad ibn Muḥammad al-Nūrī.

Qushayrī al- see Abū l-Qāsim al-Qushayrī.

Rābiʿah al-ʿAdawiyyah (d. 185/801) the most famous woman mystic in Islam (see *EI2* 8:334–36 and Knysh, *Islamic Mysticism*, 26–32).

Rūdhbārī, Abū ʿAlī Aḥmad al- (d. 322/934) an early Sufi of Baghdad and a companion of al-Junayd (see Karamustafa, 21–22, 106).

Ruwaym ibn Aḥmad (d. 303/915) a Sufi and companion of al-Junayd (see Schimmel, 59).

Sahl al-Tustarī (d. 283/896) a Sufi, scholar and author whose works include a commentary on the Qur'an (see *EI2* 8:840–41).

Sarī al-Saqaṭī al- (d. 251/865) a Sufi of Baghdad and uncle to al-Junayd (see Knysh, *Islamic Mysticism*, 50–52).

Sarrāj al- see ʿAbd Allāh ibn ʿAlī al-Tamīmī Abū Naṣr al-Sarrāj.

Shādhilī al- see Abū l-Ḥasan al-Shādhilī.

Shaqīq al-Balkhī (d. 195/810) an ascetic and early Sufi (see Knysh, *Islamic Mysticism*, 32–35).

Shiblī, Abū Bakr al- (d. 334/946) a Sufi and former student of al-Junayd known for his statements on love and for his eccentricities. He was also a friend of al-Ḥallāj (see Knysh, *Islamic Mysticism*, 64–66).

Suhrawardī, al- see ʿUmar al-Suhrawardī.

Sulāmī al- (fl. fifth/tenth century) a Sufi quoted by al-Sulamī.

Sulamī, Abū ʿAbd al-Raḥmān al- (d. 412/1021) wrote extensively on Sufism. His works include a commentary on the Qur'an entitled *The Truths of Qur'anic Commentary* (*Ḥaqā'iq al-tafsīr*), and *The Generations of Sufis* (*Ṭabaqāt al-ṣūfiyyah*), an important source on the lives and sayings of early Muslim ascetics and mystics (see *EI2* 9:811–12, and Knysh, *Islamic Mysticism*, 125–27).

Sumnūn (d. ca. 300/912) an ecstatic Sufi known for his all-consuming love of God (see, Knysh, *Islamic Mysticism*, 63–64).

Ṭabarānī, Sulaymān ibn Aḥmad al- (d. 360/971) a scholar who composed a number of works on hadith, including *The Great Collection* (*al-Muʿjam al-kabīr*) and *The Middle Collection* (*al-Muʿjam al-awsaṭ*) (see *EI2* 10:10–11).

Ṭabarī al- see Muḥammad ibn Jarīr al-Ṭabarī.

Ṭalq ibn Ḥabīb (d. 90/708) an early Muslim ascetic (see al-Iṣfahānī, 3:63–66).

Thābit al-Banānī (d. 127/744) a scholar of hadith (see al-Dhahabī, 5:220–25).

Thawbān (d. 54/674) a freed slave of the prophet Muḥammad who related hadith about him (see al-Dhahabī, 3:15–18).

Tirmidhī, Muḥammad ibn ʿĪsā al- (d. 279/892) author of *The Collection of Sound Traditions* (*al-Jāmiʿ al-Ṣaḥīḥ*), also known as *The Traditions of al-Tirmidhī* (*Sunan al-Tirmidhī*), a canonical collection of Sunni hadith (see *EI2* 10:546).

ʿUbādah ibn al-Ṣāmit (d. 45/665) a companion of the prophet Muḥammad (see al-Dhahabī, 2:5–11).

Ubayy ibn Kaʿb (d. ca. 22/643) a scribe for the prophet Muḥammad and an early authority on the Qur'an (see *EI2* 10:764–65; al-Iṣfahānī, 1:250–56; Ibn al-ʿImād, 1:32–33).

ʿUmar ibn al-Khaṭṭāb (d. 23/644) the third caliph of Islam, legendary for his piety (see *EI2* 10:818–21).

ʿUmar al-Suhrawardī (d. 632/1234) an influential Sufi and author of a number of mystical writings including his popular guide *The Gifts of Gnosis* (*ʿAwārif al-maʿārif*) (see Knysh, *Islamic Mysticism*, 195–207).

ʿUqbah ibn ʿĀmir (d. ca. 58/678) a companion of the prophet Muḥammad (see Ibn al-ʿImād, 1:64).

ʿUthmān ibn Maysarah I was unable to find information on this figure.

Uwaymir ibn Zayd al-Anṣārī, Abū l-Dardāʾ (d. 32/652) a companion of the prophet Muḥammad and later a judge in Damascus (see al-Dhahabī, 2:335–53).

Uways al-Qaranī (d. ca. 37/657) a "companion" of the prophet Muḥammad; though the two never met, according to tradition, they communicated telepathically. In the Sufi tradition, Uways represents those mystics who gain mystical enlightenment directly from the spirit of the deceased Muḥammad and without any other spiritual guide (see Schimmel, 28).

Wāsiṭī al- see Muḥammad ibn Mūsā al-Wāsiṭī.

Wuhayb ibn al-Ward (d. 153/770) a Muslim ascetic (see al-Iṣfahānī, 8:140–61).

Yaḥyā al-ʿUrmawī, Muḥyī al-Dīn (fl. ninth–tenth/fifteenth–sixteenth century) a spiritual master of ʿĀʾishah al-Bāʿūniyyah and a member of the ʿUrmawī branch of the Qādiriyyah Sufi order (see Homerin, "Living Love," 213–14).

Yaḥyā ibn Muʿādh al-Rāzī (d. 258/872) a Sufi and preacher (see Knysh, *Islamic Mysticism*, 92–93).

Yūsuf al-Bāʿūnī (d. 880/1475) father of ʿĀʾishah al-Bāʿūniyyah and a scholar of Shāfiʿī jurisprudence who held the office of chief judge in Damascus (see Homerin, "Living Love," 212–13).

Bibliography

Anṣārī, ʿAbd Allāh al-. *Kitāb Manāzil al-sāʾirīn*. Beirut: Dār al-Kutub al-ʿIlmiyyah, 1988.

Arberry, Arthur J., trans. *The Doctrine of the Ṣūfīs* by Muḥammad al-Kalābādhī. Cambridge: Cambridge University Press, 1977.

Bāʿūniyyah, ʿĀʾishah al-. *Dīwān Fayḍ al-faḍl wa-jamʿ al-shaml*. Edited by Mahdi Asʿad ʿArrār. Beirut: Dār al-Kutub al-ʿIlmiyyah, 2010.

———. *Fatḥ al-mubīn fī madḥ al-Amīn*. Edited by Ḥasan Muḥammad Rabābiʿah. Amman: Wizārat al-Thaqāfah, 2008.

———. *Al-Mawrid al-ahnā fī al-mawlid al-asnā*. MS 639 (Shiʿr Taymūr). Cairo: Dār al-Kutub al-Miṣriyyah, n.d.

———. *Al-Muntakhab fī uṣūl al-rutab fī ʿilm al-taṣawwuf*. Microfilm 13123 of MS 318 (Taṣawwuf Taymūr). Cairo: Dār al-Kutub al-Miṣriyyah, 1071/1661.

———. *Al-Qawl al-ṣaḥīḥ fī takhmīs burdat al-madīḥ*. Edited by Ḥasan Muḥammad Rabābiʿah. Amman: Wizārat al-Thaqāfah, 2009.

Behrens-Abouseif, Doris. *Mamluk and Post-Mamluk Metal Lamps*. Cairo: Institut Français d'Archéologie Orientale, 1995.

Bly, Robert. *The Eight Stages of Translation*. Boston: Rowan Tree Press, 1983.

Damīrī, Muḥammad al-. *Ḥayāt al-ḥayawān*. 2 vols. Cairo: Muṣṭafā al-Bābī al-Ḥalabī, 1978.

Dhahabī, Muḥammad al-. *Siyar aʿlām al-nubalāʾ*. 23 vols. Beirut: Muʾassasat al-Risālah, 1981.

Douglas, Elmer H., trans. "Ibn al-Sabbagh's *Durrat al-Asrar wa Tuhfat al-Abrar*." In *The Mystical Teachings of al-Shadhili*, edited by Ibrahim Abu-Rabi. Albany: State University of New York Press, 1993.

Encyclopaedia of Islam, 1st ed. Edited by M. Th. Houtsma et al. 9 vols. Leiden: Brill, 1913–38.

Encyclopaedia of Islam, 2nd ed. Edited by H. A. R. Gibb et al. 11 vols. Leiden: Brill, 1954–2009.

Encyclopaedia of Islam Three. Edited by Marc Gaborieau et al. Leiden: Brill, 2007–.

Encyclopaedia of the Qur'an. Edited by Jane Dammen McAuliffe. 5 vols. Leiden: Brill, 2001–6.

Ghazālī, Muḥammad al-. *Iḥyā' 'ulūm al-dīn*. 4 vols. Cairo: 'Īsā al-Bābī al-Ḥalabī, 1957.

———. *Al-Munqidh min al-ḍalāl*, edited by 'Abd al-Ḥalīm Maḥmūd. Cairo: Dār al-Kutub al-Ḥadīthah, 1965.

Glassé, Cyril. *The Concise Encyclopedia of Islam*. San Francisco: Harper & Row, 1989.

Graham, William A. *Divine Word and Prophetic Word in Islam*. The Hague: Mouton, 1977.

Grunebaum, Gustave E. von. *Muhammadan Festivals*. New York: Olive Branch Press, 1988.

Guillaume, A., trans. *The Life of Muhammad*. London: Oxford University Press, 1955.

Holland, Muhtar, trans. *Sufficient Provision for Seekers of the Path of Truth* by 'Abd al-Qādir al-Jīlānī. 5 vols. Hollywood, FL: Al-Baz Publishing, 1995–97.

Homerin, Th. Emil. "'Ā'ishah al-Bā'ūniyyah (d. 1517)." In *Essays in Arabic Literary Biography II: 1350–1850*, edited by Joseph Lowry and Devin Stewart, 21–27. Wiesbaden: Harrassowitz, 2010.

———, trans. *Emanations of Grace: Mystical Poems by 'Ā'ishah al-Bā 'ūnīyah (d. 923/1517)*. Louisville, KY: Fons Vitae, 2011.

———. "Living Love: The Mystical Writings of 'Ā'ishah al-Bā'ūnīyah." *Mamlūk Studies Review* 7, no. 1 (2003): 211–34.

———. "'Recalling You, My Lord': 'Ā'ishah al-Bā'ūnīyah on *Dhikr*." *Mamlūk Studies Review*. Forthcoming.

———. *'Umar Ibn al-Fāriḍ: Sufi Verse, Saintly Life*. New York: Paulist Press, 2001.

———. "Writing Sufi Biography: The Case of 'Ā'ishah al-Bā'ūnīyah (d. 923/1517)." *Muslim World* 96, no. 3 (2006): 389–99.

Ibn al-'Arīf, Abū l-'Abbās. *Maḥāsin al-majālis*. Arabic text with English translation by William Elliot and Adnan K. Abdulla. [Amersham]: Avebury Publishing, 1980.

Ibn al-Fāriḍ, 'Umar. *Naẓm al-sulūk (al-Tā'iyyah al-kubrā)*. In *Dīwān Ibn al-Fāriḍ*, edited by Guiseppe Scattolin. Cairo: Institut Français d'Archéologie Orientale, 2004.

Ibn al-Ḥanbalī al-Ḥalabī, Muḥammad. *Durr al-ḥabab fī ta'rīkh a'yān Ḥalab*. Edited by Maḥmūd al-Fākhūrī and Yaḥyā 'Abbārah. Damascus: Wizārat al-Thaqāfah, 1973.

Ibn al-'Imād, 'Abd al-Ḥayy. *Shadharāt al-dhahab fī akhbār man dhahab*. 12 vols. in 6. Cairo: Maktabat al-Qudsī, 1931.

Ibn 'Aṭā' Allāh al-Iskandarī, Aḥmad. *Laṭā'if al-minan*. Cairo: Maktabah al-Qāhirah, 1979.

Ibn Khallikān, Aḥmad. *Wafayāt al-a'yān*. Edited by Iḥsān 'Abbās. 8 vols. Beirut: Dār al-Thaqāfah, 1968.

Ibn Ṭūlūn, Muḥammad. *Al-Qalā'id al-jawhariyyah fī ta'rīkh al-Ṣāliḥiyyah*. Edited by Muḥammad Aḥmad Duhmān. 2 vols. Damascus, 1980.

Iṣfahānī, Abū Nu'aym al-. *Ḥilyat al-awliyā'*. 10 vols. in 5. Reprint, Beirut: Dār al-Kutub al- 'Arabiyyah, 1980.

Jacobi, Renate. "Ibn al-Mu'tazz: Dair 'Abdūn. A Structural Analysis." *Journal of Arabic Literature* 6, no. 1 (1975): 35–56.

Jīlānī, 'Abd al-Qādir al-. *Kitāb al-Ghunyah*. 2 vols. in 1. Cairo: Maṭba'at Muḥammad 'Alī Sabīḥ, 1940.

Kaḥḥālah, 'Umar. *Mu'jam al-mu'allifīn*. 15 vols. in 8. Damascus: al-Maktabat al-'Arabiyyah, 1957.

Kalābādhī, Muḥammad al-. *Al-Ta'arruf li-madhhab ahl al-taṣawwuf*. Beirut: Dār al-Kutub al- 'Ilmiyyah, 1980.

Karamustafa, Ahmet T. *Sufism: The Formative Period*. Berkeley: University of California Press, 2007.

Keeler, Annabel, and Ali Keeler, trans. *Tafsīr al-Tustarī*. Louisville, KY: Fons Vitae, 2011.

Knysh, Alexander, trans. *Al-Qushayri's Epistle on Sufism*. Reading, UK: Garnet, 2007.

———. *Islamic Mysticism: A Short Introduction*. Leiden: Brill, 2000.

Losensky, Paul, trans. *Farid ad-Din 'Aṭṭār's Memorial of God's Friends*. New York: Paulist Press, 2009.

Munāwī, Muḥammad al-. *Al-Kawākib al-durriyyah*. Edited by ʿAbd al-Ḥamīd Ṣāliḥ Ḥamdān. 4 vols. in 2. Cairo: al-Maktabah al-Azhariyyah li-l-Turath, n.d.

Qadḥāt, Muhammad ʿAbd Allāh al-. *ʿĀʾilat al-Bāʿūnī*. Amman: Wizārat al-Thaqāfah, 2007.

Qushayrī, Abū l-Qāsim al-. *Laṭāʾif al-ishārāt*. Edited by Ibrāhīm Basyūnī. 3 vols. Cairo: al-Hayʾah al-Miṣriyyah al-ʿĀmmah li-l-Kitāb, 1981.

———. *Al-Risālah al-Qushayriyyah*. Edited by ʿAbd al-Ḥalīm Maḥmūd and Maḥmūd ibn al-Sharīf. 2 vols. Cairo: Dār al-Kutub al-Ḥadīthah, 1972–4.

———. *Sharḥ asmāʾ Allāh al-ḥusnā*. Edited by Aḥmad ʿAbd al-Munʿim and ʿAbd al-Salām al-Ḥilwānī. Cairo: Maṭbaʿat al-Amānah, 1969.

Petry, Carl. *Twilight of Majesty*. Seattle: University of Washington Press, 1993.

Rabābiʿah, Ḥasan. *ʿĀʾishah al-Bāʿūniyyah: shāʿirah*. Irbid, Jordan: Dār al-Hilāl li-l-Tarjamah, 1997.

Renard, John, trans. *Knowledge of God in Classical Sufism*. New York: Paulist Press, 2004.

Roberts, Nancy, trans. *The Subtle Blessings in the Saintly Lives of Abu Al-Abbas Al-Mursi & His Master Abu Al-Hasan* by Ibn ʿAṭāʾ Allāh al-Iskandarī. Lousiville, KY: Fons Vitae, 2005.

Sakhāwī, Muḥammad al-. *Al-Ḍawʾ al-lāmiʿ*. 12 vols. in 6. Cairo: Maktabat al-Qudsī, 1934.

Sarrāj, ʿAbd Allāh al-. *Kitāb al-Lumaʿ fī al-taṣawwuf*. Edited by ʿAbd al-Ḥalīm Maḥmūd and Ṭāhā ʿAbd al-Bāqī Surūr. Cairo: Dār al-Kutub al-Ḥadīthah, 1960.

Schimmel, Annemarie. *Mystical Dimensions of Islam*. Chapel Hill: University of North Carolina Press, 1975.

Smith, Margaret. *Studies in Early Mysticism in the Near and Middle East.* Oxford: Oneworld, 1995.

Stern, M. S., trans. *Al-Ghazzali on Repentance.* New Delhi: Sterling Publishers, 1990.

Suhrawardī, ʿUmar al-. *ʿAwārif al-maʿārif.* Cairo: Maktabat al-Qāhirah, 1973.

Sulamī, Muḥammad al-. *Ṭabaqāt al-ṣūfiyyah.* Edited by Nūr al-Dīn Shuraybah. Cairo: Maktabat al-Khānjī, 1986.

———. *Ḥaqā'iq al-tafsīr.* Edited by Sayyid ʿUmrān. 2 vols. Beirut: Dār al-Kutub al-ʿIlmiyyah, 2001.

Watt, W. Montgomery, trans. *The Faith and Practice of al-Ghazālī.* Oxford: Oneworld, 1998.

Further Reading

ʿAlāwī, Fāris Aḥmad al-. *ʿĀʾishah al-Bāʿūniyyah al-Dimashqiyyah.* Damascus: Dār Maʿadd li-l-Ṭibāʿah wa-l-Nashr wa-l-Tawzīʿ, 1994.

Homerin, Th. Emil, trans. *Emanations of Grace: Mystical Poems by ʿĀʾishah al-Bā ʿūnīyah (d. 923/1517).* Louisville, KY: Fons Vitae, 2011.

Karamustafa, Ahmet T. *Sufism: The Formative Period.* Berkeley: University of California Press, 2007.

Knysh, Alexander. *Islamic Mysticism: A Short Introduction.* Leiden: Brill, 2000.

Petry, Carl. *Twilight of Majesty.* Seattle: University of Washington Press, 1993.

Rababiʿah, Ḥasan. *ʿĀʾishah al-Bāʿūniyyah: shāʿirah.* Irbid, Jordan: Dār al-Hilāl li-l-Tarjamah, 1997.

Index

About the NYU Abu Dhabi Institute

The Library of Arabic Literature is supported by a grant from the NYU Abu Dhabi Institute, a major hub of intellectual and creative activity and advanced research. The Institute hosts academic conferences, workshops, lectures, film series, performances, and other public programs directed both to audiences within the UAE and to the worldwide academic and research community. It is a center of the scholarly community for Abu Dhabi, bringing together faculty and researchers from institutions of higher learning throughout the region.

NYU Abu Dhabi, through the NYU Abu Dhabi Institute, is a world-class center of cutting-edge research, scholarship, and cultural activity. The Institute creates singular opportunities for leading researchers from across the arts, humanities, social sciences, sciences, engineering, and the professions to carry out creative scholarship and conduct research on issues of major disciplinary, multidisciplinary, and global significance.

About the Translator

Th. Emil Homerin is Professor of Religion in the Department of Religion & Classics at the University of Rochester, where he teaches courses on Islam, classical Arabic literature, and mysticism. Homerin completed his Ph.D. with honors at the University of Chicago and has lived and worked in Egypt and Turkey for a number of years. Among his many publications are *Emanations of Grace: The Mystical Verse of ʿĀʾishah al-Bāʿūnīyah* (2011), *Passion Before Me, My Fate Behind: Ibn al-Fāriḍ and the Poetry of Recollection* (2011), *The Wine of Love & Life: Ibn al-Fāriḍ's al-Khamrīyah and al-Qayṣarī's Quest for Meaning* (2005), *Ibn al-Fāriḍ: Sufi Verse & Saintly Life* (2001), and *From Arab Poet to Muslim Saint* (2nd revised edition, 2001). Homerin has been the recipient of grants from the Mrs. Giles Whiting Foundation, the Fulbright Foundation, the American Research Center in Egypt, and the National Endowment for the Humanities. He has also received a number of awards including the American Association of Teachers of Arabic Translation Prize, the Golden Key Honor Society's recognition for his contributions to undergraduate education, the G. Granyon & Jane W. Curtis Award for Excellence in Teaching, the University of Rochester's Teacher of the Year Award, and the Goergen Award for Distinguished Achievement and Artistry in Undergraduate Education.

The Library of Arabic Literature

Classical Arabic Literature
Selected and translated by Geert Jan Van Gelder

A Treasury of Virtues, by al-Qāḍī al-Quḍāʿī
Edited and translated by Tahera Qutbuddin

The Epistle on Legal Theory, by al-Shāfiʿī
Edited and translated by Joseph E. Lowry

Leg over Leg, by Aḥmad Fāris al-Shidyāq
Edited and translated by Humphrey Davies

Virtues of the Imām Aḥmad ibn Ḥanbal, by Ibn al-Jawzī
Edited and translated by Michael Cooperson

The Epistle of Forgiveness, by Abū l-ʿAlāʾ al-Maʿarrī
Edited and translated by Geert Jan Van Gelder and Gregor Schoeler

The Principles of Sufism, by ʿĀʾishah al-Bāʿūnīyah
Edited and translated by Th. Emil Homerin

The Expeditions, by Maʿmar ibn Rāshid
Edited and translated by Sean W. Anthony

Two Arabic Travel Books
Accounts of China and India, by Abū Zayd al-Sīrāfī
Edited and translated by Tim Mackintosh-Smith
Mission to the Volga, by Ahmad Ibn Faḍlān
Edited and translated by James Montgomery

Disagreements of the Jurists, by al-Qāḍī al-Nuʿmān
Edited and translated by Devin Stewart

Consorts of the Caliphs, by Ibn al-Sāʿī
Edited by Shawkat M. Toorawa and translated by the Editors of the Library of Arabic Literature

What ʿĪsā ibn Hishām Told Us, by Muḥammad al-Muwayliḥī
Edited and translated by Roger Allen

The Life and Times of Abū Tammām, by Abū Bakr al-Ṣūlī
Edited and translated by Beatrice Gruendler

CPSIA information can be obtained
at www.ICGtesting.com
Printed in the USA
BVHW051650281122
652956BV00023B/379

9 781479 829248